# IWO JIMA
## 1945

# IWO JIMA
# 1945

## ANDREW RAWSON

First published 2012
This edition published 2015

Spellmount, an imprint of
The History Press
The Mill, Brimscombe Port
Stroud, Gloucestershire, GL5 2QG
www.thehistorypress.co.uk

British Library Cataloguing in Publication Data.
A catalogue record for this book is available from the British Library.

ISBN 978 0 7509 6520 0

Typesetting and origination by The History Press
Printed in India

# CONTENTS

# INTRODUCTION

On 7 December 1941, Japanese planes attacked Pearl Harbor in the Hawaiian Islands and bases in the Philippines, bringing the United States of America into the Second World War. The first naval battle took place in May 1942, when Allied ships prevented a Japanese fleet taking control of the seas north of Australia. In the four-day Battle of the Coral Sea the Allied forces suffered heavy losses, but they achieved their objective of thwarting the Japanese invasion plans.

Admiral Isoroku Yamamoto wanted to lure the US Navy into battle to get the upper hand in the Pacific. It was clear that a new style of naval warfare was developing, one in which the aircraft carrier played the leading role instead of the battleship. Technological advances in aerial warfare meant that planes could track down and destroy enemy ships long before the fleets saw each other.

Allied code breakers had broken the Japanese naval code by late May 1942 and when they discovered that Yamamoto intended to capture Midway Island, halfway between Japan and Hawaii, US carriers sailed towards it looking to outmanoeuvre their adversaries. Contact was made on 4 June and in the battle that followed four Japanese carriers were destroyed or damaged, resulting in a decisive US Navy victory. Midway would later be seen as a turning point in the Pacific War.

While the Japanese had been stopped in the Eastern Pacific, they were still on the offensive in the Western Pacific, advancing in the Solomon Islands and in New Guinea. But they had been stopped by September 1942 and the Allies counterattacked later in the year. General William Slim's British and Indian XIVth Army was also holding its own in Burma.

US Marines had landed on Guadalcanal in the Solomon Islands in August 1942 but it took a six-month-long deadly battle of attrition to clear it. The stubborn Japanese defence was a taste of what was to come in the Allied island hopping campaign, as they moved slowly across the Pacific towards the Japanese homeland. Islands had to be invaded, secured and then turned into air and naval bases ready for the next stage of the campaign. While many islands were captured, others – such as Truk, Rabaul and Formosa – were bypassed and bombed into submission.

The invasion of the tiny Tarawa Atoll in the Gilbert Islands in November 1943 was a bloody experience for the Marines but they learnt many lessons about amphibious landings that were applied at Iwo Jima fifteen months later. At the same time, President Franklin D. Roosevelt, Prime Minister Winston Churchill and Generalissimo Chiang Kai-shek met in Cairo to agree a strategy to defeat Japan. While America was gearing up its industrial capacity for war, equipping not only its own armies but that of China, the Japanese Armed Forces were suffering because of the country's lack of industry and resources.

While the United States Navy and Marines were advancing slowly across the Pacific, the Imperial Japanese Army struck back in the India-Burma-China Theatre. While Operation *U-Go*, an offensive into India in March, was stopped at Kohima and Imphal, Operation *Ichi-Go*, a couple of months later, struck deep into China to attack Allied airfields.

The invasion of Saipan in the Marianas Islands on 15 June 1944 was the next step in the Eastern Pacific and over 125,000 Army troops and Marines would eventually be involved in the battle for the island. Virtually every available Japanese ship was ordered to the area but the air attacks on Fifth Fleet, starting on 19 June, were a complete disaster. The Japanese Navy lost three aircraft carriers and 450 planes in the two-day battle while the US Navy only lost 130 planes; most of them crashed while trying to land on their carriers. The Japanese carrier fleet never recovered from what became known as the Great Marianas Turkey Shoot.

General Douglas MacArthur then began his invasion of the Philippines Islands in the southwest Pacific; over 600 Japanese ground-based planes were destroyed trying to stop it. The Japanese Navy tried next and the four-day Battle of Leyte Gulf in October 1944 became arguably the largest naval battle in history; it was also the first time that Japanese pilots carried out kamikaze attacks, crashing their planes into carriers and battleships in a desperate attempt to sink them. Instead three Japanese carriers were sunk and a fourth was disabled on 24 October; another was sunk the following day, ending the Japanese Navy's ability to carry out attacks. It left Sixth Army free to expand its beachhead on Leyte and by the end of December the island was secure.

The rest of the Philippines operations followed, with an amphibious assault of Mindoro in December and Luzon in January; by 3 February US troops were in the capital, Manila. Luzon would become the largest campaign of the Pacific War while the invasion of Mindanao in April would complete the conquest of the Philippines.

The Allied offensives in Burma continued throughout 1944 and American troops linked up with Chinese troops in the north in January. To the south, Japanese troops had withdrawn to a defensive line along the Irrawaddy river but the British XIVth Army crossed it on a broad front in February.

By the time V Amphibious Corps landed on the shores of Iwo Jima on 19 February 1945, Imperial Japan's Armed Forces were falling back on all fronts. Only this time American troops were stepping onto Japanese soil and there was no doubt about it, General Tadamichi Kuribayashi and his troops would fight to the last man to stop the US Marines taking it.

# TIMELINES

## The Pacific War before Iwo Jima

**1944**

| | |
|---|---|
| **15 June** | US Marines invade Saipan in the Mariana Islands. |
| **15/16 June** | The first bombing raid against Japan since April 1942. |
| **19 June** | Climax of the 'Marianas Turkey Shoot' when US carrier-based fighters shoot down 220 Japanese planes; only 20 American planes are lost. |
| **8 July** | Japanese troops withdraw from Imphal. |
| **19–27 July** | US Marines invade Guam in the Marianas. |
| **24 July** | US Marines invade Tinian. |
| **8 August** | US troops complete the capture of the Mariana Islands. |
| **15 September** | US troops invade Morotai and the Paulaus. |
| **20 October** | US Sixth Army invades Leyte in the Philippines. |
| **23–26 October** | The Battle of Leyte Gulf results in a decisive US Navy victory. |

## 1944

| 25 October | First suicide air (Kamikaze) attacks made against US warships around Leyte. |
| 11 November | Iwo Jima bombarded by the US Navy. |
| 15 December | US troops invade Mindoro in the Philippines. |
| 17 December | US Army Air Force establishes 509th Composite Group and it starts practising how to drop an atomic bomb. |

## 1945

| 3 January | General MacArthur is placed in command of all US ground forces and Admiral Nimitz in command of all naval forces ready to assault Iwo Jima, Okinawa and Japan. |
| 9 January | US Sixth Army invades Lingayen Gulf on Luzon in the Philippines. |
| 3 February | US Sixth Army enters Manila. |
| 16 February | US troops recapture Bataan in the Philippines. |
| 19 February | V Amphibious Corps invade Iwo Jima. |

# The Battle for Iwo Jima

## 1945

| 19 February | 4th and 5th Marine Divisions land on Iwo Jima's southwest shore. Mount Suribachi is isolated and parts of Airfield 1 are captured; 30,000 Marines are ashore by nightfall. |
| 21 February | 4th Division clear Airfield 1. Japanese make Kamikaze attacks against the fleet off the coast of Iwo Jima; carrier *Bismark Sea* sunk and carrier *Saratoga* damaged. |
| 23 February | Marines reach the top of Mount Suribachi and raise the Stars and Stripes. |
| 24–28 February | 5th Division advance along the north coast towards Hill 362-A. |

**1945**

| | |
|---|---|
| | 3rd Division cross Airfield 2 and take Hill Peter and Hill 199-0. |
| | 4th Division encounter the Meat Grinder near Minami village. |
| **1–5 March** | 5th Division capture Hill 362-A and Nishi and advance towards Kita. |
| | 3rd Division seize Airfield 3 and Hill 357. |
| | 4th Division encounter the Meat Grinder near Minami village. |
| **4 March** | The first B29, *Dinah Might*, makes an emergency landing on the island. |
| **6–10 March** | 5th Division capture Kita and Hill 362-B and then close in on Kitano Gorge. |
| | 3rd Division capture Hill 362-C and advance rapidly to the east coast. |
| | 4th Division seize Higashi village but cannot take the Meat Grinder. |
| **11–16 March** | 5th Division close in on Kitano Gorge in the north of the island. |
| | 3rd Division clear Cushman's Pocket east of Motoyama village. |
| | 4th Division clear organised resistance south of Higashi. |
| **17–24 March** | 5th Division clear the final pocket of resistance in Kitano Gorge. |
| | 3rd Division search tunnels and caves across the island. |
| **26 March** | Operation *Detachment* declared complete after 35 days; General Schmidt and V Amphibious Corps leave the island. |
| **12 April** | The last Marine units leave Iwo Jima. |

## The Pacific War after Iwo Jima

| | |
|---|---|
| 3 March | The fall of Manila in the Philippines. |

## 1945

| | |
|---|---|
| **10 March** | US Eighth Army invades Mindanao in the Philippines. |
| **1 April** | US Tenth Army invades Okinawa. |
| **7 April** | P-51 Mustangs based on Iwo Jima escort B-29s over Japan for the first time. |
| **12 April** | President Roosevelt dies; he is succeeded by Harry S. Truman. |
| **8 May** | Victory in Europe Day. |
| **25 May** | US Joint Chiefs of Staff approve Operation *Olympic*, the invasion of Japan, scheduled for 1 November. |
| **9 June** | Japanese Premier Suzuki announces Japan will fight to the end. |
| **18 June** | Japanese resistance ends on Mindanao in the Philippines. |
| **22 June** | Japanese resistance ends on Okinawa. |
| **10 July** | 1000 bomber raids begin against Japan. |
| **14 July** | The first US Navy bombardment of the Japanese home islands. |
| **16 July** | First atomic bomb successfully tested in the United States. |
| **26 July** | Atomic bomb 'Little Boy' delivered to Tinian Island in the South Pacific. |
| **6 August** | First atomic bomb dropped on Hiroshima. |
| **8 August** | USSR declares war on Japan and then invades Manchuria. |
| **9 August** | Second atomic bomb is dropped on Nagasaki; Emperor Hirohito and Japanese Prime Minister Suzuki decide to seek an immediate peace. |
| **14 August** | Japanese accept unconditional surrender. |
| **29 August** | US troops land near Tokyo. |
| **2 September** | Formal Japanese surrender ceremony on board the USS *Missouri* in Tokyo Bay. |
| **8 September** | General MacArthur enters Tokyo. |

# HISTORICAL BACKGROUND

## Strategic Planning

As early as September 1943 the Joint War Planning Committee met in Washington to discuss plans for the campaign against the Japanese homeland. The Central Pacific Forces had first to neutralise the Caroline Islands so that new sea and air bases could be established; only then could attacks be launched against the Japanese Navy. The Army Air Force also wanted air bases on the Mariana Islands so their new long-range B-29 Superfortress bombers could start bombing mainland Japan.

The Committee identified the capture of one of the Nanpo Islands, midway between the Marianas and Tokyo, as an objective for early 1945. The islands were a vital part of the Japanese outer defences and the largest island in the Volcano Island group, Iwo Jima, was singled out as a key objective. Long-range fighters could then use the island's airfields to escort the bombers to Japan; returning damaged bombers could also land on the island.

In March 1944 the invasion of the Marianas was scheduled for 15 June and it would be the first stage in the advance towards the Japanese homeland.

At the end of June a paper entitled 'Operations Against Japan Subsequent to Formosa' proposed advancing from the Mariana

Islands to the Nanpo Islands in April 1945. On 12 August the Joint War Planning Committee submitted an outline plan for the invasion of Iwo Jima to the Joint Staff Planners. It listed the following advantages of taking the island:

1. It would take a strategic outpost from the Japanese.
2. Fighter planes could provide air cover for the new bases on the Marianas.
3. Fighter planes would also provide protection for bombers heading for Japan.
4. Bombers could use the island for staging attacks on Japan.

The US Armed Forces continued their operations across the Pacific throughout the summer of 1944. Saipan, Tinian and Guam were taken, clearing the Marianas by the end of August. While the Japanese Navy Air Service suffered heavily, the US Air Force went from strength to strength as new air bases were built. The continued successes convinced the US High Command that they

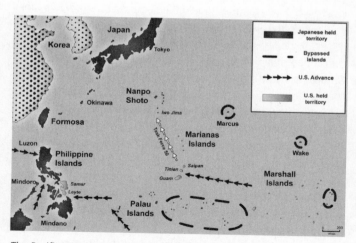

*The Pacific War at the end of 1944 involved simultaneous attacks on the Philippine Islands and the Marianas Islands.*

| Codename | Operations | Tentative Target Date |
|----------|-----------|----------------------|
| *Forager* | Capture of Saipan, Guam and Tinian | 15 June 1944 |
| *Stalemate* | Capture of Palau | 8 September 1944 |
| *Insurgent* | Occupation of Mindanao | 15 November 1944 |
| *Causeway* | Capture of Southern Formosa and Amoy | 15 February 1945 |
| *Induction* | Capture of Luzon | 15 February 1945 |

could take any island in the Pacific if sufficient naval, amphibious and shore-based air forces were made available. It meant that an attack on Iwo Jima had become a case of when, not if.

Joint Staff Planners presented the Joint Logistics Committee with its plans for the invasion of Iwo Jima by September, asking for three divisions to be ready for 15 April 1945. Admiral Chester W. Nimitz told Lieutenant General Holland M. Smith, Commanding General of the Fleet Marine Force, Pacific, to keep the 2nd and 3rd Marine Divisions ready in the Marianas as a reserve for the invasion of Formosa; they would then be used to attack Iwo Jima.

However, the Navy, Army, and Army Air Force commanders were all reconsidering the need for the invasion of Formosa. Admiral Nimitz had originally wanted bases in Formosa ready to strike the Chinese coast but recent Japanese gains in the area made him change his mind. Meanwhile, both Lieutenant General Robert C. Richardson Jr, Commanding General, Army Forces, Pacific Ocean Areas, and Lieutenant General Millard F. Harmon, Commanding General of the Army Air Forces, Pacific Ocean Areas, wanted to strike Iwo Jima instead of Formosa.

Admiral Nimitz, Admiral Ernest J. King (Commander, US Navy and Navy member of the Joint Chiefs of Staff), Admiral Raymond A. Spruance (Commander, US Fifth Fleet) and Lieutenant General Simon B. Buckner (Tenth US Army Commander and Commander of the Formosa Landing Force) met late in September in San Francisco to make the decision. The meeting illustrated that there were insufficient troops for the Formosa and southeast China operations. The War Department was also refusing to increase troop numbers in the Pacific until the war in Europe was over. Instead, Admiral King explained that there were enough forces for a different strategy. Iwo Jima in the Nanpo Islands would be taken first in January 1945; fighter support could then be provided for the B-29s raiding Tokyo. The capture of Okinawa Island in the Nansei Islands (also called Ryukyu Islands) would provide a staging area for the invasion of the Japanese mainland.

Admiral King returned to Washington and the Joint Chiefs of Staff approved the change in strategy. They issued a new directive to Admiral Nimitz in which he was told to prepare for the following operations:

1. Provide fleet cover and support for the attack on Luzon; target date 20 December 1944.
2. Occupy one or more of the Nanpo Islands; target date 20 January 1945.
3. Occupy one or more of the Nansei Islands, target date 1 March 1945.

On 9 October 1944 Admiral Nimitz told General Holland M. Smith (nicknamed 'Howling Mad'), to prepare for an invasion of Iwo Jima.

The Joint War Plans Committee issued a paper called 'Operations for the Defeat of Japan' on 18 October outlining the advantages of capturing Iwo Jima:

1. It would establish sea and air blockades.
2. It would allow B-29 bombers to carry out air attacks on the Japanese mainland.
3. It would contribute to the destruction of Japanese naval and air power.
4. It would pave the way for the eventual invasion of Japan.

Planning for the invasion of Iwo Jima could now begin in earnest.

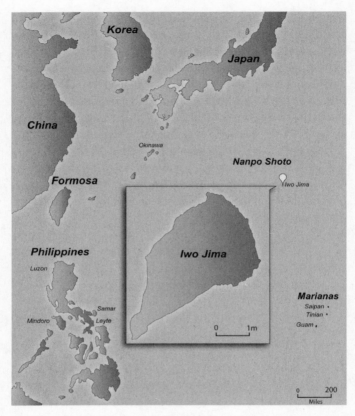

*Iwo Jima was in the Nanpo Shoto Islands, south of Japan. It was also halfway between the airbases in the Marianas Islands and Tokyo.*

Airbases on the Marianas become operational in November 1944 and B-29 bombers immediately began bombing mainland Japan, in particular the capital, Tokyo. News of the raids gave the American people and servicemen a morale boost but plane and crew losses were high, far too high. If a plane was damaged by enemy action over Japan or suffered a malfunction, the crew had to ditch in the Pacific Ocean where their chances of being rescued were zero. Although the raids had to continue, the US Air Force was desperate for a staging airfield along the flight route, and Iwo Jima was the place. Not only could fighter squadrons join the bombers en route to Tokyo, crippled bombers could land on it.

## Operational Planning

Planning for Iwo Jima continued throughout October but by mid-November it was clear that the timetable of operations had to be changed. The interval between the invasion of Luzon on 20 December and Iwo Jima on 20 January did not give time to switch shipping from one area to the other. Admiral Nimitz recommended delaying the attack on Iwo Jima (Operation *Detachment*) to 3 February while the invasion of Okinawa (Operation *Iceberg*) was rescheduled for 15 March.

The campaign to clear Leyte in the Philippines was also taking far longer than expected owing to the arrival of two new Japanese divisions on the island and the atrocious weather. General Douglas MacArthur, Supreme Commander of the Southwest Pacific Area,

*Troops and equipment come ashore on Luzon Island, the largest of the Philippine Islands. (NARA-111-SC-200008)*

had to postpone the assault on Luzon to 9 January 1945, in turn delaying the invasion of Iwo Jima. At the beginning of December Admiral Nimitz recommended delaying Operations *Detachment* and *Iceberg* to 19 February and 1 April 1945 respectively; the Joint Chiefs agreed.

## Planning Operation *Detachment*

Admiral Nimitz's staff published a preliminary report of the invasion of Iwo Jima on 7 October so planning could begin. Operation *Detachment*'s objectives were to extend US armed forces control over the Western Pacific while maintaining military pressure against Japan. The capture of the island and its airbases were also outlined as part of the overall strategy for the defeat of Japan. Admiral Nimitz's directive also specified the four commanders for the operation:

1 Operation: Commander Admiral Raymond A. Spruance, USN.
2 Joint Expeditionary Force: Commander Vice Admiral Richmond Kelly Turner, USN.
3 Joint Expeditionary Force Second in Command: Rear Admiral Harry W. Hill, USN.
4 Expeditionary Troops Commander: Lieutenant General Holland M. Smith, USMC.

General Smith received Admiral Nimitz's directive on 9 October and his staff immediately set to work planning the invasion. Fifth Fleet and V Amphibious Corps had cooperated before during the capture of the Gilberts, the Marshalls and the Marianas, and all levels of staff were used to working together. Responsibilities were distributed as follows:

Commanding General, Pacific Ocean Areas

Responsible for coordinating all aspects of the Pacific war; land, sea and air.

| Commanding General, Army Air Forces, Pacific Ocean Areas | Responsible for the long range bombing campaigns, either to support invasions or against the Japanese homeland. |
| --- | --- |
| Commander Fifth Fleet | Coordinate naval gunfire support before the invasion, during the landing and during the battle. |
| Commander Amphibious Forces, Pacific | Organise the transfer of troops, vehicles and equipment to the island during the landing and the battle. |
| Commander Service Force, Pacific | Organise the delivery of supplies and ammunition to the beachhead. |
| Commander Air Force, Pacific | Organise bombing raids by land-based planes, particularly before the invasion. |

Major General Harry Schmidt, commander of V Amphibious Corps, was in turn appointed Commanding General of the Landing Force. Schmidt's staff were responsible for preparing the Marine aspect of invasion, knowing that they had the Headquarters, Fleet Marine Force, Pacific, at their disposal.

3rd, 4th and 5th Marine Divisions had been assigned as V Amphibious Corps' Landing Force. 3rd Division had just captured Guam and it was resting and refitting on the island. 4th Division had just taken Saipan and Tinian and it was resting and refitting at its base on Maui in the Hawaiian Islands. Iwo Jima would be 5th Division's first battle but many combat-experienced troops had been transferred to it to help it complete training on Hawaii Island.

V Amphibious Corps Headquarters moved to Pearl Harbor on Oahu Island, in the Hawaii chain on 13 October 1944 to facilitate planning, and six days later Schmidt issued an outline plan. The following day, General Holland Smith, the Commanding General of Fleet Marine Force, Pacific, issued troop assignments to General Schmidt.

As the various staffs worked together to finalise the planning for the invasion of Iwo Jima, Schimdt's original plan evolved to accommodate information gathered from aerial intelligence reports. The various headquarters published their final drafts for Operation *Detachment* on the following dates:

| | |
|---|---|
| **25 November** | Commander-in-Chief, US Pacific Fleet and Pacific Ocean Areas, Operation Plan No. 11-44 |
| **23 December** | V Amphibious Corps, Operation Plan No. 3-44 |
| **27 December** | Joint Expeditionary Force, Operation Plan No. A25-44 |
| **31 December** | Fifth Fleet, Operation Plan No. 13-44 |

By the time Admiral Spruance assumed command of all forces assigned to Central Pacific Task Force on 26 January 1945, all elements of Operation Plan 11-44 were being developed.

*As V Amphibious Corps made its final preparations for Iwo Jima, Sixth Army was advancing across Luzon. Huge plumes of smoke rise above Manila's docks as the battle for the city begins. (NARA-111-SC-200052)*

# THE ARMIES

## Commanders

### General Holland Smith

General Smith, or 'Howling Mad' as he was known, was Commander of the Amphibious Force, Atlantic Fleet, in December 1941 and responsible for training several divisions in amphibious landings. He transferred to command the Amphibious Corps, Pacific Fleet, in August 1942. The organisation was later known as V Amphibious Corps and it moved to Pearl Harbor in September 1943 to begin planning for the Gilberts campaign. Smith was still in command when it was renamed Fleet Marine Force, Pacific, in August 1944.

## Major General Harry Schmidt

Schmidt was Assistant to the Commandant of the Marine Corps from January 1942 to August 1943. He then commanded 4th Marine Division during the capture of Roi-Namur in the Battle of Kwajalein and in the invasion of Saipan. In July 1944, he took command of V Amphibious Corps and led it through the invasion and capture of Tinian Island.

## General Tadamichi Kuribayashi

In December 1941, Kuribayashi was appointed Chief of Staff of the Japanese 23rd Army in time for the invasion of Hong Kong. He was promoted to lieutenant general as commander of the 2nd Imperial Guards Division, a training division, in 1943. On 27 May 1944, he transferred to the 109th Division and two weeks later was ordered to defend Iwo Jima in the Bonin Islands chain believing that 'Japan has started a war with a formidable enemy and we must brace ourselves accordingly.'

Kuribayashi arrived on the island on 19 June 1944, having had an audience with Emperor Hirohito. After surveying the island's defences he set about planning new ones inland, eventually connecting the 5000 caves with 11 miles of tunnels. He believed

that 'America's productive powers are beyond our imagination' and wanted to turn Iwo Jima into a fortress. He realised he could not hold Iwo Jima forever but was prepared to fight a battle of attrition. He expected to die and on 5 September he wrote to his wife: 'It must be destiny that we as a family must face this. Please accept this and stand tall with the children at your side. I will be with you always.'

# US Marines

## Weapons

The Marine wore the 1941 pattern utility uniform, a simple loose-cut two-piece uniform made of sage green cotton herringbone twill. It was called either utilities or dungarees but never fatigues, the US Army word for uniform. The jacket had three flapless pockets while the trousers had four; the arrangement depended on which manufacturer made them. The M1 steel helmet was covered with a camouflage cloth which had a reversible brown/green coloration. The later version had slits for foliage, something that was not needed on Iwo Jima. Leggings were worn over the boots but they were often discarded because they could be difficult to put on and were uncomfortable to wear.

A US Marine carried his equipment and personal belongings in a three-part olive drab M-1941 Haversack that could be arranged in five different ways: light marching, marching, field marching, transport and field transport. The upper section carried the rations, poncho and clothes needed in combat while the lower section contained extra shoes and utilities. The exterior of the upper pack had loops and tabs for attaching a bayonet, shovel, extra canteen and first-aid pouch; a bedroll could be folded around the top. The belt suspenders completed the haversack. The harsh Pacific environment quickly faded and then rotted the uniform and equipment.

Officers were issued with either Colt M1911 or M1917 .45 calibre revolvers. The rank and file Marines were armed with the M1 Garand, which had a high rate of fire thanks to its gas operated rotating bolt system. The semi-automatic rifle fired .30–60 Springfield ammunition from the 8-round internal magazine and could also fire fragmentation, anti-tank and smoke grenades using a spigot attachment and special ammunition. The shorter M1 Carbine was issued to officers, NCOs and other specialists who benefited from carrying this shorter, compact weapon; it fired a 7.62mm round from a 15- or 30-round box.

The M1A1/M1928 Thompson submachine gun could fire over 600 .45 ACP rounds a minute from 20- or 30-round stick magazines and they were often issued to scouts, NCOs and patrol leaders. Delays in production meant that only a limited number of M3 submachine guns, or 'Grease Guns' were available. Some men were issued with the Winchester M12 Trench Gun, a six-round pump action shot gun for close quarter combat. The MkII Fragmentation grenade and smoke and white phosphorous variants were used in great numbers in the close-quarter fighting, while the Ka-Bar knife could be used in a tight corner.

The M1918 Browning Automatic Rifle, or BAR, had a high rate of fire and the .30 rounds it fired from a round box magazine had a high stopping power. It could be mounted on a bipod for increased accuracy and the trigger man could choose either automatic or semi-automatic fire. The M1917 Browning machine gun was a heavy, tripod-mounted weapon and its four-man crew used it in a semi-static role. It was water cooled and the belt-fed mechanism could fire up 600 .30 rounds a minute. The M1919 Browning Machine Gun was an air-cooled tripod-mounted weapon with a crew of two; it also had a maximum rate of fire of 600 rounds a minute.

The M2-2 flamethrower was an excellent weapon for clearing pillboxes. It could fire a single ten-second burst or five two-second bursts of burning fuel from its two back-pack style canisters. Typically, each squad had one and the while one man operated the trigger, the other operated the valves. The Japanese feared the flamethrower and snipers kept a look out for the distinctive profile of the fuel tanks or for a bright burst of flame so they could engage the team. While there were few Japanese tanks to engage on Iwo Jima, the M1A1 bazooka was another useful weapon for engaging emplacements; it had a two-man crew, one man to fire and one to load.

# Kit

The 75mm pack howitzer was a versatile weapon known as the 'Little Dynamite', which could be manhandled into areas that heavier artillery could not reach. It could be used to carry out direct firing against bunkers up to a range of around 500 metres or for indirect fire against targets up to 9000 metres away. The Marine division artillery battalions were equipped with the M2A1 (M101A1) 105mm Howitzer, which was capable of firing high explosive rounds to a range of 11,200 metres. The Corps artillery battalions had the M114 155mm Howitzer, capable of firing to a range of 14,600 metres.

The Marine tank battalions were equipped with Sherman M4A3 (medium) tanks armed with the 75mm M3/L40 gun, which could fire armour piercing or high explosive rounds, and one .05 calibre and two .03-6 calibre Browning machine guns. They weighed 30.3 tonnes and had 53mm of armour at the front, 63mm at the side and 40mm at the back; they rarely reached their top speed of 30mph on Iwo Jima. Sherman tanks mounting flamethrowers were particularly effective and burning fuel could be fired approximately 91 metres; each tank carried 300 gallons of fuel, which gave 150 seconds of flames. The tanks' air intakes and exhausts were modified with chimneys so they could drive off the landing ships and through shallow water onto the beach. M3 Gun Motor Carriages were half tracks, mounting a 75mm gun, and they were used as mobile anti-tank guns to attack emplacements.

Everything had to be brought to Iwo Jima by sea and the huge logistics operation involved a wide range of ships and landing craft. The Landing Ship, Tank (LST) was 106 metres long, 16.8 metres wide and could either carry ten tanks and fifteen vehicles or 160 officers and men; it had a crew of 104. The Landing Ship, Medium (LSM) was 62 metres long, 10 metres wide and could either carry five tanks, six LVTs (amphibious armoured carriers), nine DUKWs (amphibious trucks) or 54 officers and men; it had a crew of 58.

*A Landing Ship Tank delivers Sherman tanks to the shore. Some bogged down in the soft sand, a few hit mines and others were hit by Japanese artillery; the few lucky survivors were welcomed by the Marines. The air and exhaust intakes which allowed tanks to beach in shallow water can be seen. (NARA-127-GW-109825)*

The Landing Vehicle Tracked (LVT(A)-1), was an armoured amphibious vehicle used to ferry men from the Landing Ships to the shore. The 'amtrack' as it was widely known was 7.95 metres long, 3.25 metres wide and could carry 18 men or 2000kg of supplies; it had a three man crew. The LVT(A)-4 variant mounted a turret with a 75mm Howitzer. The DUKW was a six-wheeled drive amphibious truck used to ferry artillery from the Landing Ships to the shore. It was widely known as the 'duck', and was 9.4 metres long, 2.5 metres wide and could carry 2.3 tonnes or 12 men; it only had one crewman. Once ashore, ammunition and supplies were taken inland by the Clever-Brooks amphibian trailer, which could carry a 3.5-ton load, or the M-29C Light cargo carrier (Weasel), which hauled a half-ton load.

*An amtrack crew get their final instructions from one of the control boats supervising 4th Division's assembly area before heading towards the beach. (NARA-127-GW-110134)*

## Tactics

The Marines were virtually always on the offensive and the fighting tended to follow a steady pattern. The Japanese would watch and wait in their camouflaged bunkers and caves until the Marines were fixed firmly in their sights. After everyone went to ground, spotters would locate the Japanese position while armoured dozers cut a road forward so the tanks could move into position, guided by the Marines. While the flame tanks sprayed the area with burning liquid, the Shermans fired 75mm rounds and their machine guns at the bunker aperture or cave mouth. Flamethrowers and tank flamethrowers were found to be the best weapons for clearing the Japanese out of their bunkers and caves.

Once the bunker was temporarily silenced, the assault team rushed forward to make sure no one was left alive inside. The Marines could then renew their advance but they had to be wary of Japanese soldiers opening fire from a new, hidden position. Demolition teams had to check the area, searching the caves and pillboxes for signs of life; they rarely saw any. Progress was slow and dangerous and advances were often measured in metres.

The engineers landed alongside the assault troops and they had to carry out a variety of perilous tasks. They had to use flamethrowers and explosives to blast open or seal pillboxes and caves. They also had to probe for mines in the volcanic ash or use explosives to carve routes through the rock for tanks. 5th Engineer Battalion described two methods of advancing through a minefield when tanks were not available:

Mines had to be removed by hand, under fire; or equipment had to be run into the minefield until it was blown up, then removed and the process repeated until a path through the minefield was opened. The former method was slow, tedious, and exposed highly trained specialists to high casualties. The latter method was slow, and costly in armoured dozers and tanks.

The artillery found it difficult to locate and then silence Japanese mortar, artillery and rocket batteries. Corps and division observation and intelligence officers pooled their information with aerial observers for the best results. The Japanese made excellent use of the rough terrain and camouflage to hide their weapons and they held their fire until they would have the maximum impact on the Marines' advance, usually when they were in an exposed position. The Regimental headquarters then had to quickly establish where the Japanese guns were, either from the men on the ground or from the observer planes circling overhead.

The information had to be transmitted to the artillery batteries or fleet ships so that counter battery fire could be arranged as quickly as possible. It meant that the men on the ground often had to wait hours under fire until the Japanese guns were silenced.

An Intelligence Officer with 4th Marine Division makes it clear that combined arms attacks were the only way to advance. He also shows how the Japanese often withdrew to a new position when the Marines were closing in:

> Our Battalion CO has coordinated his direct support weapons and delivers a concentration of rockets, mortars and artillery. Our tanks then push in, supported by infantry. When the hot spot is overrun we find a handful of dead Japs and few if any enemy weapons. While this is happening, the enemy has repeated the process and another sector of our advance is engaged in a vicious fire fight, and the cycle continues.

*This flamethrower team is making sure that no one is left alive; two men cover the bunker with their rifles while a third squirts burning fuel into the aperture. (NARA-127-GW-111008)*

The Japanese were masters of infiltration at night and towards the end of each day every commander had to assess his unit's progress. If necessary, some were ordered to withdraw to 'tie in' their flanks and form a solid defensive front. Marines would dig in for the night, set up their support weapons, establish communications and post lookouts. They would then have to keep watch all night, raising the alarm if anything suspicious was seen.

## The Japanese

The Japanese soldier wore the Type 98 pattern yellowish-khaki, or mustard, two part uniform which faded in the tropical climate. He had a wool uniform for winter and a cotton one for summer; he could wear a khaki cotton shirt in warm conditions. The long trousers or pantaloons were secured over the ankle boots with spiral wound woollen puttees and tapes.

Officers had to buy their own uniforms so style and quality varied and colours ranged from tan to dark green. A Type 3 officer's uniform was introduced in 1943 in various shades of green and it was a cheap cut of material with cuff insignia. Jackets could be worn over a white or light green shirt, and the uniform was completed with a black or green tie.

Most officers and men wore cloth field caps with a leather or cloth peak and they came in various shades of green ranging from grey-green to a dark green. Some wore the Type 92 dome helmet but it was made of poor quality steel and was little use against shrapnel; others wore the Type 92 cork version tropical helmet.

Officers bought their own revolvers and while some had the woefully inadequate old Type 26 double action revolver, some had the newer Type 4 or Type 14 recoil spring action revolvers. The Type 94 was a lightweight recoil operated, locked breech action weapon. Many officers bought Western revolvers due to the unreliability of the Japanese models. Officers were also armed with the Shin Gunto, or New Army Sword, which was both a badge of rank and a weapon.

The Japanese soldier was armed with the Type 99 Short Rifle, a bolt action weapon which fired a 7.7mm Arisaka cartridge from a 5-round internal magazine. The Type 2 rifle grenade launcher was attached to the rifle and a blank cartridge or wooden bullet propelled the 30mm or 40mm rounds. Many soldiers used the Type 99 sniper version to good effect in Iwo Jima's rough terrain. They also carried the Type 99 hand grenade or the Type 4 Ceramic grenade. The ceramic version had a porcelain or terracotta body and they had been introduced because the Japanese armaments industry could not produce enough steel grenades.

A few soldiers might have been armed with submachine guns but production was limited and few were available. The Type 100/40 could fire 450 8mm Nambu rounds a minute but it had a complicated design and often jammed. The Type 100/44 was a modified version that had resolved many of the problems and it could fire 800 rounds a minute.

The Type 96 light machine gun could fire 700 7.7mm Arisaka rounds a minute. It was an air-cooled, gas-operated machine gun and was fed by a 30-round top mounted curved box magazine. The Type 92 heavy machine gun could fire a 7.7mm round up to 400 rounds a minute but it used a strip cartridge rather than a belt system and had a tendency to jam. This heavy weapon was tripod mounted and the three-man team usually operated it from a fixed position. The lighter Type 1 heavy machine gun had been introduced in 1941 but it too was usually fired from fixed positions.

Japanese soldiers often used the Type 89 grenade launcher and although it was called the knee launcher by the Marines, it was a mortar type weapon with short tube supported on a rod and base. The operator held it against the ground and dropped the grenade down the tube and the timer was designed to explode the grenade above the ground. It was conveniently portable, easily concealed, had a rapid rate of fire and could be fired out of caves or slit trenches. The Type 97 81mm mortar had a range of 2800 metres while the modified Type 99 had the recoil mechanism removed to make it lighter. Type 94 90mm and Type 96 150mm mortars had a range of 4000 metres and both had Type 97 versions, again with the recoil mechanism removed to make them lighter. They were often used in fixed positions on Iwo Jima, as were a range of mortars over 150mm calibre. Although the Japanese Army had a small number of flamethrowers, they were rarely used in the defensive role.

## Kit

The Japanese deployed a number of different artillery pieces and while the Type 94 75mm mountain gun could be broken down and carried as a pack artillery piece, the Type 95 75mm Field Gun needed towing. The Type 92 100mm cannon and Type 4 150mm howitzer would have been virtually immobile during the battle. There were a variety of fortress cannons and howitzers deployed in bunkers and fortified caves along the coast, the majority overlooking the landing beaches.

Both the Type 97 Chi-Ha tank armed with a 47mm gun and the Type 95 Ha-Go armed with a 37mm gun, were deployed on Iwo Jima. Both types were small and only had thin armour no more than 25mm thick. They were no match for the Marines' Shermans and they were often half buried or hidden in gullies in the hope that they could shoot at close range.

The 26th Tank Regiment was sailing from Japan to Iwo Jima in July 1944 when its convoy was intercepted. On 18 July the *Nisshu Maru* was torpedoed near Chichi Jima by the American submarine, USS *Cobia*, and while only two of the 600 crew members were drowned, all 28 tanks were lost. It was December before 22 replacement tanks arrived.

## Tactics

Japanese tactics changed as the battle progressed. Before the invasion, General Kuribayashi focused his attentions on driving the Marines off the island. Previous experience had shown that

*Japanese tanks were designed to operate in jungle areas and were much smaller and lighter than their American counterparts. This crew had hidden their machine out of sight ready to catch the advancing Marines in the flank. (NARA-127-GW-143230)*

the US Navy and Air Force could devastate fortifications along the beach. Instead positions covering the beach would be camouflaged and remain silent until the waves of assault troops were ashore. They would open fire as soon as the Marines moved off the beach.

While no beach or underwater obstacles were used, the beach area was protected by mines and anti-tank ditches. Dozens of camouflaged bunkers, pill boxes and spider holes, all linked by trenches or tunnels, covered the approach to Airfield 1. Heavier artillery pieces, field guns and mortars were positioned on the slopes of Mount Suribachi and the Quarry, overlooking the flanks of the beach. They could either fire at the troops as they moved inland or at the landing craft while they unloaded troops and equipment along the shoreline. Kuribayashi was hoping that the devastating crossfire from hidden positions would force the Marines to evacuate the beachhead before nightfall.

However, V Amphibious Corps was able to secure a beachhead and force its way inland. They found that the Japanese were dug in everywhere, having spent months building and camouflaging their defensive positions. Each one had been carefully positioned to cover likely avenues of advance and provide interlocking fields of fire.

*The Marines needed to use every trick in the book to outwit their cunning enemy. Here they are trying to fool a sniper into giving his position away by raising a helmet on a rifle. (NARA-127-GW-113649)*

# The Armies

The Japanese soldiers hid underground during barrages and airstrikes and dragged their support weapons to the surface as soon as they ended, ready to engage the advancing Marines. They wanted to draw the Marines in and engage them in close combat, so that they could not use their heavy support weapons or call down artillery or air strikes. It meant that ground had to be captured in close combat with the aid of tanks, flamethrowers and demolitions. Many Japanese positions only fell after vicious hand-to-hand fighting. When weapons became clogged with volcanic ash soldiers resorted to fighting with rifle butts, knives, hand grenades, picks and entrenching tools.

If the Japanese were trapped, they refused to surrender, choosing to fight to the death or commit suicide. It meant that the Marines suffered heavy casualties in the deadly war of attrition. Often the Japanese soldier would evacuate his position at the last moment, withdrawing along tunnels or caves to a new hiding place. 4th Division's Intelligence Officer summarised the hit and run tactics used by the Japanese:

> The enemy remains below ground in his maze of communicating tunnels throughout our preliminary artillery fires. When the fire ceases he pushes Observation Posts out of entrances not demolished by our fires. Then choosing a suitable exit he moves as many men and weapons to the surface as he can, depending on the cover and concealment of that area, often as close as 75 yards from our front. As our troops advance toward this point he delivers all the fire at his disposal, rifle, machine-gun, and mortar. When he has inflicted sufficient casualties to pin down our advance he then withdraws through his underground tunnels most of his forces, possibly leaving a few machine gunners and mortars.

Sometimes the Marines worked all day long, destroying pillboxes and caves, with hardly a shot being fired; then the Japanese emerged after dark to attack.

To begin with the Japanese artillery and heavy mortars were dug in and camouflaged while their crews selected and calculated the ranges to likely targets. With the Marines controlling the air, it was important only to fire when necessary because a lack of transport meant it was often impossible to move a heavy weapon to a new position. Once a battery position had been spotted, it was targeted until destroyed by air strikes, naval bombardments and artillery fire. The amount of Japanese artillery fire rapidly reduced during the final stages of the battle as the Marines pushed the infantry back, capturing key observation points and battery positions.

The few Japanese tanks on the island were generally kept hidden and deployed in a semi-static role. Once they had stopped an attack, they would move to a new hidden position. Meanwhile, the Japanese soldier had to be proactive to stop tanks getting close to their emplacements, particularly the hated flame tanks. They used antitank mines and ditches to stop tanks or force them to drive in front of an anti-tank position. Close-quarter attack units also crept up on a tank and then jumped out to place charges in its tracks or against weak side or rear armour. The tactic was suicidal but acceptable to the Banzai mentality of the Japanese soldier. These close-quarter attack units were also used to infiltrate the Marine lines so that they could attack command posts, communications installations or artillery positions.

# THE DAYS BEFORE THE ASSAULT

There was a large beach on both sides of the long southern neck of the island but the American planners advised landing only on the southeast side. Prevailing northerly or north westerly winds generated rough surf on the southwest beaches, creating dangerous conditions for landing craft and amphibious vehicles. On 8 January 1945 V Amphibious Corps revised its assessment and believed that landing craft could transfer unloading operations to the southwest beaches if the wind changed direction.

The plan was for 4th and 5th Divisions to land side-by-side on the southeast beaches, with 26th Marines waiting offshore as the Landing Force reserve. 3rd Division had been slated as Expeditionary Corps reserve and it would wait off Iwo Jima's coast until ordered ashore. While the divisions had their own organic artillery, limited space on the beachhead meant that 1st Provisional Field Artillery Group would be limited to two battalions of 155mm howitzers. V Amphibious Corps would have to rely on close air support and naval gunfire to compensate for the lack of heavy artillery. 138th Anti-aircraft Artillery Group would land as soon as possible to provide protection for the beachhead.

## The Invasion Plans

Major General Keller E. Rockey's 5th Division would land on the southern section of the beach, codenamed Green and Red. Colonel Harry B. Liversedge's 28th Marines would land on the left on Green 1 Beach, advance across the narrow neck of the island and then turn southwest to cut Mount Suribachi off from the rest of the island. Colonel Thomas A. Wornham's 27th Marines would land on the right, on Red 1 and Red 2 Beaches, cross to the opposite shore and then advance northeast along the west side of Airfield 1. 1/26th and 3rd/28th Marines would be released from the division reserve when required and land on Red or Green Beaches. Colonel Chester B. Graham's 26th Marines would be ordered forward from corps reserve when necessary. Colonel Louis G. DeHaven's 14th Marines were the division artillery and gun crews would occupy designated battery positions as soon as they were captured.

Major General Clifton B. Cates' 4th Division would land on the northern section of the beach, codenamed Yellow and Blue Beaches. Colonel Walter W. Wensinger's 23rd Marines would land on Yellow 1 and Yellow 2 Beaches and advance across the west half of Airfield 1 before turning northeast towards Airfield 2. Colonel John R. Lanigan's 25th Marines would land on Blue 1 Beach and clear the rest of Airfield 1, Blue 2 Beach and the Quarry. Colonel Walter I. Jordan's 24th Marines would be called forward from 4th Division reserve when necessary and land either on Blue or Yellow Beach. Colonel James D. Waller's 13th Marines were the division artillery and gun crews would occupy designated battery positions as soon as they were captured, like the 14th.

Major General Graves B. Erskine's 3rd Division was due to be released from Expeditionary Troops Reserve on or after D-plus-1. 9th Marines would land on Yellow Beach while 21st Marines would land on Red Beach.

Aerial reconnaissance showed that the Japanese defences covering the beach had been considerably strengthened over the winter, resulting in last minute changes to the landing plans. General Schmidt wanted to extend the three-day naval bombardment based on previous bad experiences. General Smith also wanted 5th Marine Division to take Mount Suribachi quickly and 26th Marines was transferred from corps to divisional reserve while one battalion was assigned to 5th Division ready to go ashore if necessary. One of 3rd Marine Division's RCTs took 26th Marines' place in corps reserve.

The plan was for 68 LVT(A)4s (amtracks) armed with 75mm howitzers to hit the shoreline at H-Hour and drive up onto the first terrace of the beach ready to give covering fire while waves of LVTs delivered the Marines to the shore. 4th and 5th Tank Battalions

*This aerial view over the south tip of the island, looking from the west, shows how V Amphibious Corps had to develop both beaches. The area between was crammed with all manner of headquarters, logistics units, stores and medical facilities. (NARA-111-SC-206876)*

## MARINE COMBAT ORGANISATION

The acronym RCT is an American military term for the Regimental Combat Team. On Iwo Jima a Combat Team was composed of a Marine regiment and all the attached combat and support units, including tanks platoons, specialist engineers, logistics units and medical facilities. While the Regiment was responsible for carrying out the divisional orders in its sector, the attached units could be transferred between regiments at short notice.

would wait offshore in Landing Ships until called forward, to avoid congestion on the beach. A similar plan to land on the western beaches was prepared in case the wind changed direction. A small island off the west coast called Kangoku Rock would be also be checked out and used as an artillery site if suitable.

## Gathering Intelligence

A lot of intelligence about Iwo Jima was already available when V Amphibious Corps began planning for Operation *Detachment*. Data had been gathered for air strikes by carrier planes in June and July 1944 and it was used to prepare preliminary situation maps and beach studies; however, more detailed information was needed. Documents captured on Saipan in June 1944 gave General Schmidt's staff an idea of the Japanese Order of Battle on Iwo Jima. However, additional troops had been moved onto the island ready to repel the invasion and V Amphibious Corps intelligence section had to collect new information.

A total of 371 aerial photography sorties were flown over Iwo Jima during the weeks that followed and they charted the progress of the Japanese defences as well as the damage done by bombing. The staffs of the Amphibious Forces, Pacific, and the Fleet Marine Force, Pacific, produced a Joint Situation Map on 6 December 1944 and at the end of January 1945 their photo interpretation officers met on Guam to collate information. A few days later they produced the 'Joint Enemy Installation Map', identifying all known Japanese positions on the island.

The Navy also wanted to know more about Iwo Jima, and the submarine *Spearfish* had been observing the coast since early December 1944. The commander spied on the island and took photos of the shoreline, concluding that while tractors could cross the beach, wheeled vehicles would struggle to get off it. He also noted gasoline drums had been half buried close to the waterline, ready to be set on fire as soon as the Marines stepped ashore.

The overall conclusion was that the Japanese had nine battalions deployed in extensive field works across the island. Major General Osuka had divided his defences into four sectors,

---

# JAPANESE DEPLOYMENT

| | |
|---|---|
| Mount Suribachi Sector | 312th Independent Infantry Battalion |
| Southern Sector | 309th Independent Infantry Battalion |
| Western Sector | 311th Independent Infantry Battalion, 1st Company 26th Tank Regiment |
| Eastern Sector | 314th Independent Infantry Battalion, 3rd Company 26th Tank Regiment |
| Northern Sector | 3rd Battalion, 17th Independent Mixed Regiment, 2nd Company 26th Tank Regiment |
| Airfield 1 | 1st Battalion, 145th Infantry |

Each sector was reinforced by Naval Land Force units, coastal defence troops and anti-aircraft units.

---

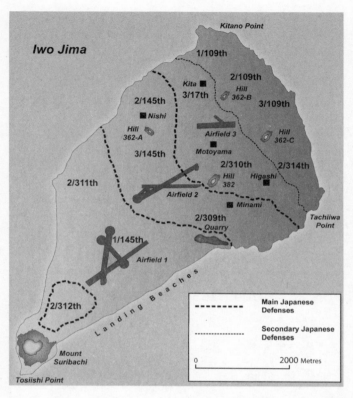

*The Japanese defences on Iwo Jima and the deployment of the main infantry units.*

with one infantry battalion manning each sector; a fifth battalion was deployed around the coast. The expectation was that the remaining four battalions would be held in reserve ready to counterattack. If the counterattack failed the survivors would probably fall back to the high ground at the northeast end of the island and fight to the last man.

The Japanese had concentrated a large part of their efforts in covering the beaches, deploying artillery and mortars at each end. Anti-tank ditches had been dug to funnel tanks onto minefields while more mines protected bunkers and pillboxes. It was clear from the aerial photographs that the number of fortifications had more than doubled between December 1944 and February 1945, in spite of the air raids. It also appeared that the Japanese had prepared a new defensive line across the centre of the island. It ran diagonally from Hiraiwa Bay on the northwest coast in a south-easterly direction to the high ground north of the East Boat Basin.

The additional fortifications meant only one thing: that there were far more troops on Iwo Jima than anticipated. The Japanese had been reinforcing Iwo Jima by sea and on 6 January intelligence officers increased their estimate of the garrison to over 13,000 troops. The new outline of the Japanese Order of Battle was as follows:

- 4720 men of 2nd Mixed Brigade, 109th Division, commanded by Major-General Koto Osuka
- 3950 men of 145th Infantry Regiment, commanded by Colonel Masuo Ikeda
- 2 anti-tank gun battalions and a mortar battalion with 1650 men
- A detachment of the 26th Tank Regiment with 350 personnel, 30 medium and 10 light tanks
- The Iwo Jima Naval Guard Force with 1750 men
- 400 naval airbase personnel and 700 airbase construction personnel.

Intelligence also assumed that Lieutenant General Tadamichi Kuribayashi had overall command of the Defence Sector covering the Volcano and Bonin Islands – part of the Nanpo Shoto Islands – and that he controlled it from 109th Division Headquarters on Chichi Jima. It also supposed that Major General Osuka was in charge of preparing Iwo Jima's defences.

While V Amphibious Corps always referred to Iwo Jima as 'Island X', there was a serious security breach on 22 December 1944. The *Honolulu Advertiser* printed an illustrated article on US Air Force bombing raids and noted that the target was Iwo

## FOREWARNED

Japanese submarines had shadowed Task Force 51's build up in the Marianas and reported its journey towards Ulithi to Tokyo. Japanese Imperial Headquarters was sure that Iwo Jima was the likely target. On D-10 Tokyo warned 109th Division headquarters of an imminent attack and gave the size and composition of the invasion force to General Kuribayashi.

Jima. Anyone studying operational photographs could see that the two photographs accompanying the article were of Island X. V Amphibious Corps responded by putting out information that the recent build-up of ships and troops were preparing for an attack on Formosa. It made no difference to General Kuribayashi's defensive plans; his men continued to dig themselves deep into Iwo Jima's rocky terrain.

## Logistics and Administration

A successful invasion had to be supported by a well planned logistical operation. The troops ashore had to be supplied with ammunition, food and water, while the wounded needed to be evacuated quickly. Landing Ships had to bring everything to the waters off Iwo Jima ready to be transferred to landing craft and delivered to the beach. The Marines could then haul what they needed to the front line. The same applied to evacuating the wounded, in reverse.

While Fleet Marine Force, Pacific, had prepared outline logistical plans, General Schmidt's staff began working on the details as soon as V Amphibious Corps took over. Their final plan involved three different Pacific-based logistic organisations. Fleet Marine Force's Supply Service would supply the Marines with ammunition, equipment and supplies. The US Army Forces Quartermaster would

*Once the amtracks had delivered the Marines to the shore, they were kept busy ferrying supplies to the front line and returning with injured men. Twin-mounted machine-gun turrets kept snipers at bay. (NARA-127-GW-109691)*

supply Army troops with ammunition, supplies, equipment; it would also supply rations for Marine and Army units. The Navy's Service Force would provide fuels and lubricants for all units ashore.

Supplies were delivered to Saipan and then packed onto ships; some were loaded onto amtracks and DUKWs ready to be driven ashore. During the battle they would wait offshore until the supplies were required and then be loaded onto landing craft and ferried to the beach. There were no offshore reefs, so all types of landing craft could carry supplies direct from the transports to the beach. Colonel Leland S. Swindler, the Landing Force Shore Part Commander, then had the job to make sure that 8th Field Depot coordinated the division shore parties. The danger was that stores would clutter up the shoreline, creating a dangerous logistical bottleneck and an inviting target; they had to be moved inland as soon as possible. If all else failed, V Amphibious Corps' Air Delivery Section was on standby to make emergency air drops to front-line troops.

Five Provisional Amphibian Truck Companies equipped with DUKWs had been assigned to V Amphibious Corps; 4th and 5th Marine Divisions had one each and three were Army units. Two new transport vehicles had also been made available and while the Clever-Brooks amphibian trailer could carry a 3.5-ton load, the M-29C Light cargo carrier, or Weasel, was capable of hauling a half-ton load.

There were concerns that wheeled vehicles would not be able to carry supplies off the beach and several contingency plans had been prepared. Supply pallets would be stacked on runner sleds so that tracked vehicles could drag them off the beaches. Steel matting was also provided to create temporary roads. Steel planks, called Marston matting, were normally used for temporary airstrips but hundreds had been hinged together in groups of seven, ready to be stretched out across the beach to form temporary track ways. A total of 8.5 miles of Marston matting was prepared in the Pearl Harbor Navy Yard.

Landing Ship, Mediums (LSMs) would carry five Sherman tanks each directly to Iwo Jima's beach so they could drive straight onto the shore. The tanks had been fitted with exhaust and air intake vents in case the landing ships could not get right to the beach and they had to drive a short distance through shallow water. The first tank company to land close to Mount Suribachi was carried by a Landing Ship, Dock and three much smaller Landing Craft, Tank (LCTs) transferred them to the shore.

While each division had its own organic engineer battalions, 133rd and 31st Naval Construction Battalions, known as Seabees, had been attached to 4th and 5th Divisions. Engineers would have to clear mine fields and obstacles, build roads and facilities and establish water supplies. They would also be called upon to support the Marines, using their demolition skills to destroy bunkers and emplacements. V Amphibious Corps also had a number of specialist engineer units to deal with bomb disposal and mapping.

The Japanese airfields had to be repaired and improved and work would commence as soon as they were captured. 62nd Naval Construction Battalion had to open Airfield 1 as soon as possible for observation planes and fighter aircraft while 31st Seabees would repair Airfield 2 and extend it to 7000 feet, ready to receive crippled B-29s returning from Japan.

One thing that V Amphibious Corps was sure of, there would be high casualties, both during and after the landings, and the wounded had to be evacuated and treated quickly to maintain morale. Each of the divisional medical battalions had 144 beds and V Corps had an extra medical battalion; it also had Evacuation Hospital Number 1 and 38th Field Hospital. The corps could care for 3160 casualties while 8th Field Depot could look after another 1500.

Once patients were well enough to travel, small Landing Craft, Vehicle, Personnel (LCVPs) would transfer them to one of the four LSTs that had been converted into evacuation control centres, situated a mile offshore. Patients would receive emergency treatment and their details would be logged before they were transferred via another LCVP to one of the three hospital ships, the *Samaritan*, the *Solace* and the *Bountiful*. The auxiliary hospital ships *Pinkney* and *Ozark* were also available. Casualties would then be shipped to Saipan and Guam, where 5000 beds were waiting. The plan was to evacuate the wounded directly from Iwo Jima as soon as transport planes could land on the island.

## Training and Rehearsals

All three Marine divisions trained continuously throughout the winter of 1944/45. Troops practised loading and unloading from amphibious vehicles and landing craft. They also perfected the new tactics they would be expected to use on Iwo Jima, with the emphasis on how to silence bunkers and pillboxes.

*Pole-charges, explosives strapped to a long handle, were effective for knocking out bunkers. The Marines had to work their way forward under covering fire until they were close enough to push the charge through the embrasure. (NARA-127-GW-112017)*

Towards the end of November 1944 each division received around 2500 replacement drafts and although they had basic combat skills, it was too late to integrate them into the training programme. Instead they would be used to unload stores on the beaches and help move them inland. They would join units as soon as needed to replace casualties. The late delivery of DUKWs and new M4A3 Sherman tanks also caused problems.

Troops practised loading in the Hawaiian Islands over the Christmas and New Year period before they joined the Joint Expeditionary Force at Oahu in the Hawaiian Islands. Large rehearsals

*Marines cross the forward well deck of their landing ship to take their place at the top of a cargo net. Their tiny landing craft are being lowered into the sea in the background. (NARA-127-GW-112470)*

followed between 12 and 18 January, but the LSTs could not be beached because of underwater reefs, and the DUKWs stayed onboard because they were vulnerable to corrosion after spending time in seawater. Despite the problems, the Hawaiian exercises were valuable for everyone, particularly the inexperienced 5th Division.

The final rehearsals were held in the Marianas Islands in mid February and while the Marines climbed aboard their landing craft, they did not land on the shore. Instead, the emphasis was on bringing together the different shipping and air elements. The manoeuvres allowed the Attack Force carrying the Marines (Task Force 53) to check communications and coordination with the armed landing craft of the Amphibious Support Force (Task Force 52) and the ships of the Naval Gunfire and Covering Force (Task Force 54). Once the training was over the combined elements of Fifth Fleet (Task Force 50) and Joint Expeditionary Force (Task Force 51) headed for Saipan.

## Sailing to Iwo Jima

While 5th Division loaded at Hawaii, 4th Division loaded at Maui and 3rd Division loaded at Guam; corps and garrison troops loaded into six APAs and four AKAs in the Hawaiian area. Eventually, 485 ships were loaded and heading for Saipan to assemble as Task Force 51. There were 70,000 men and around 98,000 tons of cargo on board, the largest amphibious invasion assembled so far in the Pacific. The transport squadron carrying Task Force 51 was organised into three transport divisions, one for each of the Marine divisions. Each transport division allocated four troop transports known as Auxiliary Personnel, Attack (APAs) and one cargo ship known as Auxiliary Cargo, Attack (AKA) to a transport assault division which carried the divisional troops. It also allocated one APA and one AKA to carry corps troops and their supplies.

Landing Ship, Tanks (LSTs) and Landing Ship, Mediums (LSMs) carried the assault infantry and their amtracks, the artillery and their DUKWs, as well as tanks and other mechanised equipment. The assault troops were loaded in LVTs and carried to Iwo Jima in LSMs. 4th Division had sixteen, 5th Division had thirteen; two LSMs carried Corps troops. The planners had made sure that men, equipment and ammunition would be landed together ready to go straight into action. They also saw to it that the LSMs were loaded with spare water, ammunition, rations, fuel and lubricants so that the Marines were self sufficient until their supply chain was established.

Each division had nineteen LSTs and while 3rd Division had two extra to carry its tank battalion, four carried Corps troops. The LSTs were also preloaded with spare cargo. 50 amphibian cargo trailers were also loaded and sailed on LSV *Ozark* ready to go ashore on D-Day; the *Ozark* would then serve as an evacuation hospital.

The Landing Force convoy started arriving off Saipan on 14 February and the following afternoon it started heading north with an aircraft carrier and naval ships for protection. The transports carrying RCT 21 followed two days later so that it would ready off Iwo Jima by mid morning on D-Day. The transports carried 3rd Division and RCT 9. The Expeditionary Troops' reserve followed over the next 48 hours; they would be in position 80 miles off the island by D-Day.

## The Preliminary Bombardment

By 19 February 1945 Iwo Jima had already endured the longest and most intensive aerial attack delivered in the Pacific during the Second World War. It had started with a carrier raid in June 1944 and Seventh Air Force's B-24 Liberator bombers stationed on the Marianas Islands began a six-month bombing campaign in August. The frequency and intensity of the air raids steadily increased and Marine B-25 medium bombers started their own raids in early December from new bases on the Marianas. Fighters also carried out low-level attacks, often targeting Japanese ships delivering troops and supplies to the island; 23 ships were sunk, leaving the garrison short of many essential items.

The Iwo Jima Air Support Plan began on D-20, by which time the Marianas-based Liberators were flying an average of 30 daily sorties over the island. V Amphibious Corps hoped that the intensive air raids would neutralise the Japanese airfield installations, knock out gun positions and destroy camouflage, uncovering new targets.

One point of contention between the Navy and the Marines was the duration of the preliminary naval gunfire bombardment. The original plan had a cruiser division opening the bombardment on D-8 while seven pre-Second World War battleships and six more cruisers would join in on D-3. The Marine naval gunfire specialists thought it would be insufficient based on their experiences on Tarawa, Saipan and Peleliu, where the assault troops had suffered heavy casualties on the beaches. They either wanted more ships or a longer bombardment to soften up the Japanese defences.

## AIR SUPPORT

Support Carrier Group (Task Group 52.2) had eleven escort carriers: *Sargent Bay, Natoma Bay, Wake Island, Petrof Bay, Steamer Bay, Makin Island, Lunga Point, Anzio, Bismarck Sea, Saginaw Bay* and *Rudyerd Bay*. The Group's planes carried out most of the close air support missions for the Marines until Airfield 1 was open on 8 March.

General Schmidt initially requested a ten-day bombardment by one cruiser division and three battleships but his request was denied. He reduced his request to nine days and then to four days but the naval planners insisted on only three days. Schmidt finally asked if the ships could concentrate their shelling on the landing beaches; he was turned down again.

While it appears that the Navy planners were being inflexible, they had a good reason based on the strategy they had chosen. Fast Carrier Force (Task Force 58) was scheduled to attack Tokyo at the same time as Task Force 51 approached Iwo Jima, forcing the Japanese Navy Air Service to protect the capital rather than attack V Amphibious Corps. If heavy seas or enemy action forced Task Force 58 to withdraw, the Japanese planes could head to Iwo Jima. The naval planners argued that the bombardment had to be kept to a minimum period to limit the chances of it being disrupted. The Navy was also concerned about the amount of ammunition its battleships and cruisers could carry. They would have to be resupplied if the bombardment lasted longer than three days, a dangerous activity in the middle of a battle.

By the end of January it was clear that several major support vessels would not be ready. Some were still needed in the Philippines, others were being repaired. It meant that the Navy commanders had to look for alternative ships while their planners issued a revised bombardment plan on 28 January. The new battleships *North Carolina* and *Washington* were allocated to the invasion force but while they had powerful 16-inch guns, they would not reach Iwo Jima until D-Day.

On 27 January, Admiral Spruance took over from Admiral William F. Halsey on Ulithi in the Caroline Islands and the US Third Fleet was renamed the Fifth Fleet. At the same time, Vice Admiral Marc A. Mitscher replaced Vice Admiral John S. McCain as commander of the Fast Carrier Force and it was renamed Task Force 58.

Task Forces 52 and 54 reached the Marianas on 12 February and two days later all the shore bombardment units headed for Iwo Jima. While Rear Admiral Bertram J. Rodgers' Gunfire and Covering Force (Task Force 54) controlled the battleships and cruisers, Rear Admiral William H.P. Blandy's Amphibious Support Force (Task Force 52) controlled the smaller vessels. Its Gunboat Support Units, Mortar Support Group and Rocket Support Group would target the beach defences while the Air Support Control Unit and Support Carrier Group would coordinate airstrikes. The Mine Group and Underwater Demolitions Group would carry out beach reconnaissance and destroy underwater obstacles.

On the morning of 16 February, Rear Admiral Rodgers's Naval Gunfire and Covering Force (Task Force 54) began shelling Iwo Jima. Admiral Blandy's staff on board the *Estes* (AGC 12) controlled the bombardment and its target priorities were as follows:

Priority A   Coastal guns and anti-aircraft guns which threatened ships and aircraft
Priority B   Bunkers and pillboxes threatening the Landing Force
Priority C   Caves, bivouac areas, ammunition and fuel dumps

The Task Force had three days to neutralise 724 A and B targets. It was a tall order for the 6 battleships, 4 heavy cruisers and 1 light cruiser.

Rear Admiral Alexander Sharp's Mine Sweeping Group (Task Group 52.3) led Task Force 54 to its firing positions and although they were ready to open fire at 08:00, intermittent low clouds blinded the airborne observers. Firing schedules had to be abandoned and the ships' guns only fired when there was a break in the clouds. To make matters worse, anti-aircraft fire forced observation planes to stay above 3000 feet so they could not assess the effects of the bombardment. By the end of the first day it was clear that the naval bombardment had achieved little. The overcast skies also prevented Army Air Force bombers from flying over Iwo Jima, although the planes belonging to Rear Admiral Calvin T. Durgin's Support Carrier Group (Task Group 52.2) had flown 158 sorties.

Meanwhile, planes from Admiral Mitscher's Fast Carrier Force hit the Tokyo area for two days, drawing the Japanese Air Services away from the island as planned. The carriers then headed south for Iwo Jima, aiming to be there by 19 February.

As 17 February dawned clear the three battleships, *Nevada*, *Idaho*, and *Tennessee*, sailed to within 3000 metres of the shore and opened fire. They in turn came under fire from Japanese shore batteries and both the *Tennessee* and the cruiser *Pensacola* were hit. Two hours later 12 Landing Craft LCI(G)s sailed close to the shore and fired rocket salvoes at the beaches while Underwater

*TBM-3 Avengers and FM-2 Wildcats of Composite Squadron (VC) 96 aboard USS* Rudyerd Bay *(CVE-81), circa April 1945.*

## STAYING THE COURSE

Lieutenant Herring was knocked unconscious when LCI (G) 449 was hit on 17 February. He recovered only to be wounded a second time when a mortar shell knocked out the conning station, killing or wounding most of his fellow officers. As the landing craft lurched out of control, Herring climbed into the wrecked pilot house and gave instructions to the engine room. Herring was awarded the Medal of Honor for keeping the landing craft on the firing line.

Demolition Teams swam ashore. The teams checked the surf conditions, took samples from the beach and destroyed underwater obstacles while the Japanese guns and mortars hammered the gunboats. The gunboat crews retaliated with their 40mm guns but it was a one-sided battle and they had suffered heavy casualties by the time they withdrew an hour later; nine boats had been put out of action and three had been damaged.

The *Tennessee*, *Nevada* and *Idaho* also bombarded the beach with smoke shells until the demolition teams withdrew; they suffered only one casualty. The teams went on to check the west coast beaches in the afternoon. They found suitable beach and surf conditions on both sides of the island and no underwater obstacles.

Although the Japanese gunners had drawn first blood, they had exposed their positions firing on the landing craft, and Admiral Blandy ordered all available weapons to engage the new targets. Meanwhile, heavy anti-aircraft fire still kept the Army Air Force B-24s at a high level while the carrier-based planes flew 226 combat sorties against the Japanese gun positions. But in spite of the good weather, observers believed hardly any Japanese positions had been knocked out on 17 February.

V Corps' Naval Gunfire Officer recommended a change of plan, wanting the 'maximum concentration of bombardment

## A BRAVE ATTEMPT

Kuribayashi made the following report on the demolition teams: 'We were immediately posted to our positions to make preparations for an attack, and at the same time our artillery laid down a fierce barrage. At first, both sides were firing and the continuous smoke and noise of the explosions were terrific. This lasted for 30 minutes after which the enemy without attaining its objective moved the attack to the west coast. The enemy made all of this sacrifice without attaining any results.'

[to] be placed on and near the preferred landing beaches' by four battleships and one heavy cruiser. Early the following morning, Admiral Rodgers ordered his ships to 'close [to] beach and get going.' They sailed to within 2500 metres of the shore with instructions to use up all their spare ammunition, but once again visibility was poor. Even so the *Tennessee* fired 333 rounds at the batteries on Mount Suribachi while the *Idaho* fired another 280 into the Quarry area at the north end of the beach.

The low cloud over Iwo Jima also cancelled all Seventh Air Force missions while escort carrier planes could only carry out 28 sorties. By nightfall the three-day bombardment was over and Schmidt could only hope that it had done enough to allow his Marines to survive once they were ashore. Admiral Blandy's summary report to Admiral Turner was optimistic:

Though weather has not permitted complete expenditure of entire ammunition allowance and more installations can be found and destroyed with one more day of bombardment, I believe landing can be accomplished tomorrow as scheduled if necessary. I recommend special attention, before and during landing, to flanks and east coast of island, with neutralizing fire and white phosphorus projectiles immediately available if required…

Admiral Turner agreed; the assault would go ahead as planned.

A single low-flying enemy plane flew over the fleet later that evening, dropping a bomb on the *Blessman* (APD48). The explosion caused over 30 casualties; tragically, most of them were the underwater demolition experts who had survived the hazardous beach reconnaissance missions the previous day.

The bombardment of the Japanese coastal defences began at 06:40 on 19 February 1945, and everyone noticed that the fleet had been reinforced by the *Washington*'s and *North Carolina*'s 16-inch guns. Five minutes later nine LCI(R)s fired the first of 9500 5-inch rockets at Motoyama Plateau, north of the beach. For the

*All aboard. Marines of 28th Regiment try to organise themselves as they crowd into a Higgins landing craft. (NARA-127-GW-11247)*

next 90 minutes the ships hammered the Japanese defences while the transports moved to their debarkation stations, ready to begin unloading. The rest of the support craft began moving into position at 07:30 and targeted Mount Suribachi and the high ground north of the beaches with their rockets and mortar shells. Then between 08:05 and 08:25 (H-minus-55 to H-minus 35) the fire-support ships manoeuvred into their final positions. There was a short break in the naval bombardment while 120 carrier-based planes bombed and strafed the landing beaches. The naval guns resumed firing as soon as the planes headed back to their carriers.

All around the battleships and cruisers, LSTs and transports assembled in their assigned areas before opening their bow doors or lowering their ramps. APAs began lowering the tiny LCVPs into the water and they circled while waiting their turn to receive

*As the naval bombardment reaches a crescendo, wave after wave of landing craft and amphibious vehicles head for the shore through the choppy waves; there was no turning back.*

troops. While some Marines climbed into their assigned LVTs, others clambered down the cargo nets into their landing craft.

At 07:25 the launching warning signal was given and 20 minutes later 482 amtracs loaded with the first wave of eight battalions turned towards the shore. The navy gunners set their shells for ground bursts while the rocket craft fired another salvo at the beaches and mortar boats shelled the surrounding area.

At 08:05 the naval guns stopped firing and the ships moved closer to the shore; it was time for Admiral Mitscher's Fast Carrier Force to do its bit. As the LVTs neared shore, the Marines watched as 72 fighter and bomber planes flew low overhead, strafing, firing rockets and dropping bombs. Another 48 fighters followed, dropping napalm, firing more rockets and more strafing. Admiral Rodgers' battleships resumed their bombardment as soon as the planes left the area. The naval gunners had increased the range too quickly in previous landings, resulting in excessive casualties on the beach. This time the 5-inch guns would slowly increase the range of the rolling barrage, only 400 yards in front of the Marines. It would require close coordination between the ground

*As surf batters the crowded Higgins boats, the Marines watch the Navy bombard the shore. The thought on every one's mind is will it be enough? (NARA-127-GW-111904)*

troops and the ships offshore to keep the barrage in time with the rate of advance.

General Smith was pleased to hear that all phases of the pre-H-Hour preparation were going to plan and his troops would begin landing at 09:00 as intended. There was no going back now and at 08:30 the first wave of 68 LVT(A)s began the 4000-metre journey from the line of departure. It would take 30 minutes to reach the shore, 30 minutes for the men to contemplate what might be waiting for them on and beyond the beaches. The naval commanders believed they had destroyed or neutralised most of the enemy guns overlooking the landing beaches and their approaches. The Marines were about to find out if their assessment was correct.

Gunboats firing rockets and 40mm shells were following the first wave and they turned right and left to their firing positions at the last moment. At 08:57 the naval guns switched to targets on the flanks while the planes returned, flying low as they strafed the beaches.

# SECURING THE BEACHHEAD (D-DAY TO D+7)

## D-Day, 19 February 1945

At 09:02 the first wave of LVT(A)s hit the beaches of Iwo Jima. The crews discovered that they could not drive their vehicles up the steep terraces behind the beaches; they were also too high for them to give supporting fire. As they withdrew into the water in search of inland targets, the first wave of LCVPs hit the beach and lowered their ramps, allowing hundreds of Marines to step ashore along the 3500-metre wide strip of dark volcanic sand. The time was 09:05.

For the first few minutes Japanese resistance was light and the Marines were relieved to find that there were no obstacles or minefields along the beach. Units quickly reorganised and clambered up the first terrace, finding it hard to walk as their feet sank into the volcanic ash. For a few minutes all was calm and as the first wave advanced inland, some wondered if the naval gunfire and air bombardment had subdued the Japanese. It had not. They were being watched from dozens of hidden bunkers and emplacements. Artillery and mortar crews, machine-gun teams and snipers waited with their fingers on their triggers as the Marines moved tentatively forward.

Suddenly the guns and mortars on Suribachi and the northern plateau opened fired at registered targets along the beach. At the

# Iwo Jima 1945

## V AMPHIBIOUS CORPS

The Marines came ashore as follows from left to right:

| 5th Division | Colonel Harry B. Liversedge's 28th Marines on Green Beach |
| | Colonel Thomas A. Wornham's 27th Marines on Red 1 and Red 2 Beaches |
| 4th Division | Colonel Walter W. Wensinger's 23rd Marines on Yellow 1 and Yellow 2 Beaches |
| | Colonel John R. Lanigan's 25th Marines on Blue 1 Beach |

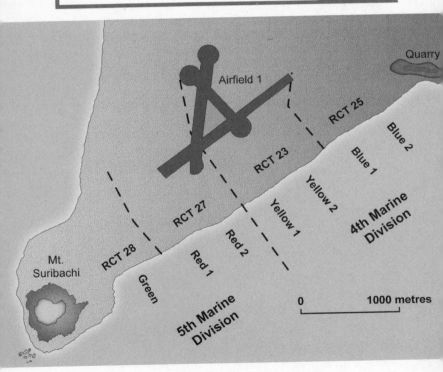

*The landing plan for the Marine Regimental Combat Teams.*

*Clear the ramps! As the coxswain slows down ready to land, bullets begin to skim the waves. With only moments to go before the ramp drops, one man bows his head and prays he will survive. (NARA-127-GW-110823)*

same time the men who had sat out the bombardment in their concealed pillboxes and caves opened fire with machine guns and rifles. In a matter of minutes the whole beachhead was under fire as the Marines scrambled for cover behind the beach terraces or in bomb craters.

Squad leaders and platoon commanders did what they could to rally their men and get them to locate the Japanese bunkers but casualties were mounting and units were disintegrating. For the time being, men took orders to advance from the nearest officer or squad leader. They engaged anything in range and little by little the Marines edged forward.

However, wave after wave of men and vehicles were coming shore, adding to the congestion and confusion along the water's edge. As jeeps and trucks bogged down in the soft sand, artillery and mortar shells rained down on the landing craft, many of which were swamped or broached on the shoreline and their crews joined the Marines in their battle to advance inland.

*Go, Go, Go! Bullets and shrapnel meet the Marines as they spill out onto the beach. RCT 26's first wave is already pinned down at the top of the sand bank and the second wave needs to find cover on the exposed beach. (NARA-127-GW-111114)*

## Cutting off Hot Rocks (D+1 to D+4)

On the left flank, 28th Marines' 1st Battalion landed first with Companies B and C abreast. Lieutenant Colonel Butterfield's men pushed inland, looking to reach the western shore as quickly as possible, but while some squads moved fast, others became pinned down in front of one of the many bunkers and pillboxes; they all suffered heavy losses. At 10:35 Company B reached the opposite shore, cutting Mount Suribachi off from the rest of the island, and Company C was soon expanding the tiny foothold.

Company A mopped up behind them and as Corporal Tony Stein's platoon advanced inland, he stood up so he could spot the Japanese guns, using his machine gun to draw their fire. He later captured a nest of pillboxes alone, killing 20 soldiers. After running out of ammunition, Stein removed his helmet and shoes and headed back to the beach for more, with a wounded man on his back. He continued his one-man rampage, carrying seven

There is nowhere to hide as the artillery and machine guns on Mount Suribachi rake the beach with bullets and shrapnel. Bodies and debris litter the shoreline while the living try to find cover and get organised. (NARA-127-GW-111156)

Despite the heavy fire, squad leaders and platoon officers begin to gather their men together, ready to advance. This group are looking for the rest of their company on Green Beach before moving towards Suribachi, codenamed Hot Rocks. (NARA-127-GW-110918)

more wounded men back as he collected more ammunition. At the end of the day he covered the withdrawal of his platoon to the company position. Stein was killed in action on 1 March and posthumously awarded the Medal of Honor.

2nd Battalion had started landing at 09:35 and Lieutenant Colonel Johnson's men found it difficult to deploy under heavy mortar and artillery fire as they turned west to face the foot of Mount Suribachi. As casualties mounted, Colonel Harry B. Liversedge called for reinforcements and although Lieutenant Colonel Shepard's 3rd Battalion was ashore by 13:00, it did not reach 2nd Battalion until late afternoon.

Lieutenant Colonel Collins' 5th Tank Battalion supported 5th Division and Company C was sent ashore to help RCT 28. The landing craft had been warned not to land on Red 1 Beach due to congestion and heavy fire so the naval officers landed on Red 2 Beach. By 14:00 the company was ashore, having lost only one tank, and the 13 Sherman tanks, two flame tanks and tankdozer crawled towards the front line in single file. A hidden anti-tank gun stood in the column's way and the Japanese crew were determined not to let them through; four tanks were hit before it was silenced.

At 11:30 General Rockey passed on General Schmidt's order to exploit weak points in the Japanese lines to RCT 28. Colonel Liversedge was hoping to attack the foot of Mount Suribachi by mid afternoon but 3rd Battalion was not ready when 2nd Battalion attacked at 16:45. Although progress was made, 2nd Battalion had to withdraw at nightfall to maintain contact with 3rd Battalion.

27th Marines landed on the 1000-metre wide strip of beach designated Red 1 and Red 2. After reorganising, E and F Companies of Major Antonelli's 2nd Battalion made good progress on the left as did Company C of Lieutenant Colonel Butler's 1st Battalion. However, Company B landed 200 metres to the left of its planned position, resulting in a delay. Butler ordered Company A to put ashore and it took over the advance, moving rapidly alongside Company C across the southern end of the airfield.

Late in the morning Colonel Thomas A. Wornham was pleased to welcome Company B, 5th Tank Battalion ashore and two platoons helped 2nd Battalion reach the west coast by mid afternoon. A third platoon of tanks joined 1st Battalion but they were unable to make much progress across Airfield 1. Lieutenant Colonel Donn J. Robertson's 3rd Battalion mopped up the area behind 2nd Battalion while Lieutenant Colonel Daniel C. Pollock's 1st Battalion, 26th Marines came ashore to take up defensive positions behind RCT 27.

As dusk approached, General Rockey ordered his two regiments to consolidate their positions and dig in for the night. Although they were nowhere near the O-1 Line, 28th Marines had isolated Mount Suribachi, and 27th Marines had reached the western shore of Iwo Jima.

While 5th Division's two assault regiments were pushing inland, Colonel Chester B. Graham's 26th Marines spent most of the day offshore. It had been released as early as 10:00 and the men were in their craft an hour later when the order to proceed to the line of departure was given. There they waited for four hours until Red 1 Beach was cleared. The battalions then landed one after another and took up defensive positions at the southern end of Airfield 1.

Reconnaissance parties belonging to Colonel James D. Waller's 13th Marines, 5th Division's artillery regiment, went ashore mid morning, only to find that their selected battery positions were still in enemy hands. DUKWs of the 5th (Marine) and 471st (Army) Amphibian Truck Companies began taking the guns ashore in the early afternoon but bulldozers and LVTs had to tow each one off the beach. Although 3rd Battalion was firing at Mount Suribachi by dusk it took until the following morning to tow and manhandle the rest of the Regiment's guns off the beach and into position. While the Marines found it relatively easy to get the 75mm pack howitzers guns into position, it required Herculean efforts to do the same for the heavier 105 howitzers.

## 4th Division Advances towards Airfield 1

Colonel Walter W. Wensinger's 23rd Marines landed on Yellow 1 and Yellow 2 Beaches on the left of General Cates' 4th Division's sector. 1st Battalion came ashore on Yellow 1 Beach and as Lieutenant Colonel Haas' Marines climbed over the terraces beyond the beach they came under heavy fire from Airfield 1. Sergeant Darrell S. Cole led his machine-gun section forward, destroying two emplacements with hand grenades on the way. When faced with another three Japanese pillboxes, he deployed his remaining machine gun and silenced the nearest one before the weapon jammed. He then advanced towards the others armed only with a pistol and grenades; he was killed after knocking out the first one. Cole's actions allowed his company to take their objective; he was awarded the Medal Honor.

Major Davidson's 2nd Battalion met the same difficulties after coming ashore on Yellow 2 Beach. Both battalions needed tanks and when the first of three LSMs of Company C, 4th Tank Battalion, approached the shore at 10:05, Colonel Wensinger was sure that his Marines would soon be on the airfield. Lieutenant Colonel Schmidt watched in horror as his first tank ashore bogged down in the soft sand, blocking the remaining four tanks on the LSM. The remaining twelve tanks came ashore without a hitch but three tanks were disabled when they ran over mines. The remaining tanks reached 1st Battalion, but heavy anti-tank fire stopped them moving beyond the embankment marking the airfield perimeter. They could not reach 2nd Battalion either because of the soft ash and the Marines were forced to attack a large strongpoint alone; it took until the late afternoon to overrun it and reach the airfield perimeter.

It was clear that 23rd Marines needed reinforcements if it was going to get to Airfield 1 and at 13:00 Major Scales was ordered to put 3/23rd Marines ashore on Yellow 1 Beach. In spite of heavy casualties on the beach, it passed through 1st Battalion and reached the airfield perimeter by nightfall. General Cates had also ordered the 1st and 2nd Battalions of Colonel Walter I. Jordan's 24th Marines ashore at 14:00. While 2nd Battalion relieved the shattered 2/23rd Marines at the airfield, 1st Battalion dug in as a reserve.

Colonel John R. Lanigan's 25th Marines landed on 4th Division's right flank on Blue 1 Beach and the southern edge of Blue 2 Beach while the Japanese watched from the quarry cliffs to the northeast. They did not watch for long and the beaches came under heavy fire as the regiment advanced in two directions. Lieutenant Colonel Mustain's 1st Battalion went quickly inland on the left, reaching the airfield before noon. Lieutenant Colonel Chambers' 3rd Battalion ran into difficulties as it set about clearing Blue 2 Beach and the quarry area. The battalion headquarters and Company L landed on 1st Battalion's beach while the rest of 3rd Battalion lost contact with 1st Battalion as it headed northeast towards the quarry.

*RCT 25 Regiment came under intense fire as soon as it advanced off Blue Beach on the right flank. While 1st Battalion crawled forward, 3rd Battalion took heavy casualties trying to reach the Quarry area. (NARA-127-GW-110108)*

## HEROISM AT THE QUARRY

The momentum of the assault on the Quarry area was threatened by heavy casualties but Lieutenant Colonel Chambers reorganised his men and inspired them to attack the critical high ground. He lost most of his officers and carried out many tasks himself during the eight-hour battle for the Quarry. Chambers was critically wounded while directing the rocket platoon's fire and was evacuated under heavy fire; he was awarded the Medal of Honor for his part in securing the beachhead's right flank.

1st Battalion also encountered difficulties as it turned north and advanced under heavy fire across Airfield 1. A second gap began to open in the Marines' line as RCT 25 wheeled sharply away from RCT 23; Colonel John R. Lanigan had to deploy reserves to fill it.

The three LSMs carrying Company A, 4th Tank Battalion were all hit on Blue 1 Beach and they had to withdraw as soon as they had unloaded. The company tank dozer was knocked out

*In spite of the intense fire and heavy casualties the Marines kept pushing inland and by nightfall they had established a solid beach head. The white tape directs them to their assembly area. (NARA-127-GW-109821)*

while it carved a road off the beach, and although the rest of the company headed inland in column, they soon ran into a minefield. The tank crews then had to fight a battle with the Japanese gunners on the cliffs while engineers quickly cleared a way forward.

In the early afternoon Lieutenant Colonel Hudson's 2nd Battalion came ashore on Blue 1 Beach and advanced through the regiment's centre aiming to take the high ground northwest of the quarry. RCT 25 renewed its attack at 14:00 and although 3rd Battalion advanced to the top of the quarry it had lost 19 officers by nightfall. Elsewhere progress was slow and casualties were high. While 1st Battalion was unable to hold the ground it had taken near Airfield 1, 2nd Battalion captured the ridge line northwest of the quarry.

By the time Colonel Lanigan joined his advance command post, 25th Marines had secured the eastern end of the beachhead and Lieutenant Colonel Vandegrift's 3/24th Battalion was in reserve. Although it would take most of the night to reorganise and evacuate casualties, Lanigan's men would be ready to renew the attack the following morning.

Reconnaissance parties belonging to Colonel Louis G. DeHaven's 14th Marines, 4th Division's artillery regiment, found that many battery positions were still in enemy hands when they went ashore. Only 1st and 2nd Battalion's DUKWs put ashore and

## FIREPOWER

The Amphibious Support Force gave fire support all day and many support vessels were hit as they fought a running battle with the Japanese coastal guns. The 606 aircraft belonging to Task Force 52 and Task Force 58 flew missions throughout the day. They fired 2254 rockets, delivered over 100 napalm bombs and dropped 274,500lbs of bombs.

*Japanese mortars, machine guns and anti-tank guns continued to hit the congested beach as landing craft brought supplies ashore. (NARA-127-GW-110271)*

by the time tractors had dragged their artillery pieces inland it was too dark to fire at observed targets.

The beach was a congested mess of men, equipment and stores and the Japanese guns shelled it mercilessly throughout the day. Only ammunition, rations, water and signal equipment were delivered on D-Day by a continuous stream of LCVPs and LCMs. Shore party teams stacked supplies above the high water mark so the landing craft could withdraw, while LVTs and Weasels worked around the clock, hauling supplies to inland dumps before returning with wounded men. Meanwhile, amtracs ferried stores directly from the LSTs to the Marines.

Unloading stopped when nightfall approached and the shore parties spent the night clearing mines and cutting routes off the beach. Meanwhile, many wounded spent the night on the beach, lying helplessly near the waterline while shells exploded around them. Most of the transports and vessels withdrew to a safe distance at nghtfall but the command ships, preloaded LSTs and hospital LSTs remained close to the beach.

By the end of D-Day neither 5th nor 4th Marine Divisions were anywhere near the O-1 Line set by V Amphibious Corps; but it was highly unlikely that the Japanese would be able to drive them back into the sea. Six Marine regiments, six artillery battalions and two tank battalions were ashore and they were holding a virtually continuous front with the few gaps covered by fire.

Although the Japanese defenders only tried one counterattack against RCT 27 during the night, they did pound the Marines' lines with mortars and artillery. They also tried to infiltrate the Marines' lines at several points but were all stopped. 1/28th Marines engaged a barge which tried to land on the west coast, killing everyone onboard.

The initial reports on casualties on D-Day were exaggerated due to the high number of men missing from their units. Many had joined the first platoon commander or squad leader they met on the beach and fought under them until nightfall. They returned to their units during the night. While the accurate casualty figures are shockingly high, they were lower than expected and V Amphibious Corps' assessments of the regiments' combat efficiency ranged from very good to excellent.

## D-DAY CASUALTIES

V Corps casualty figures for D-Day were later determined to be over 2300 – one man killed or injured for every 1.5 metres of Iwo Jima's beach.

| | |
|---|---|
| Killed in action | 501 |
| Died of wounds | 47 |
| Wounded in action | 1755 |
| Missing in action | 18 |
| Total | 2321 |

## The Battle for Hot Rocks (D+1 to D+4)

By the early morning of 20 February there were two distinct battle developing on Iwo Jima: the fight for Mount Suribachi at the southern end of the island and the advance north astride Airfield 1. General Kuribayashi had designed his defences to cope with such a situation and the Suribachi position was capable of fighting on without assistance. We will first consider the battle for Mount Suribachi.

28th Marines were in the shadow of the 500-foot-high extinct volcano and Colonel Liversedge planned to explore the base of the mountain for routes to the summit, while his artillery shelled the Japanese bunkers on the slopes above. Following a bombardment by naval guns and carrier aircraft, 2nd Battalion and 3rd Battalions attacked, even though the tanks were still waiting to be refuelled or rearmed. The mortars and artillery were also too close to target the Japanese positions, leaving the Marines reliant on their assault demolition teams to silence the enemy with flamethrowers and explosive charges. 28th Marines had hardly moved when the tanks joined the battle and they helped them advance another 200 yards before dusk.

After an uneasy night, 40 planes swooped low past Mount Suribachi on the morning of 21 February, striking targets close to RCT 28's front lines. Once again the tanks were delayed and neither 1st Battalion nor 3rd Battalion could move until they arrived; they then advanced rapidly to the base of the mountain. Both flanks then pushed forward along the shoreline, aiming to reach Tobiishi Point at the southern tip of the island. By nightfall Colonel Liversedge's men were entrenched in a semicircle at the foot of Suribachi while the Japanese in their bunkers overhead were unable to bring their guns to bear on the Marines.

While 2nd Battalion mopped up RCT 28's rear area, Private First Class Donald J. Ruhl crawled onto a bunker with his platoon guide. As they fired down on Japanese soldiers, a grenade landed next to them and Ruhl rolled on top of it to save his buddy's life.

*28th Marines prepare for the toughest task of all, the capture of Mount Suribachi. As fighters dive bomb the Japanese positions at the base of* Hot Rocks, *105mm howitzers of the 13th Marines join in the bombardment. (NARA-127-GW-110141)*

He had already made a name for himself by helping to silence a blockhouse on D-Day before risking his life to rescue a wounded Marine lying in No Man's Land the following day. Ruhl was posthumously awarded the Medal of Honor.

By 22 February, RCT 28 had been in action for 72 hours and Liversedge's Marines had had little rest and only cold rations to eat. After three days of good weather, D+3 was a miserable reminder of how quickly it could deteriorate. Cold, drizzling rain and a driving wind soaked the Marines to the skin and turned the volcanic ash into a sludge that stuck to clothing and clogged weapons.

The bitterest fighting occurred in RCT 28's centre because the tanks could not reach the area and the artillery were unable to give support. Instead the Marines used demolitions and flamethrowers to silence the bunkers at the base of Suribachi. Meanwhile, the patrols continued working their way around the mountain and they met at the southern tip of the island at 16:30. Although *Hot Rocks* had been surrounded, both patrols reported that naval gunfire and airstrikes had destroyed most of the paths up the steep slopes; the only way up was on the north face in 2nd Battalion's zone.

On the morning of 23 February, Colonel Liversedge ordered Lieutenant Colonel Johnson to investigate the path and two 3-man patrols from Companies D and F set out at 09:00. Up and up they went, meeting no Japanese on the way, and 35 minutes later they reached summit and peered into Suribachi's crater.

*Lieutenant Schrier's group pose for the camera in front of their Stars and Stripes on the summit of Mount Suribachi. All eyes turned to the top of Hot Rocks and as the Marines cheered, the vessels offshore sounded their horns. (NARA-127-GW-112449)*

## Securing the Beachhead

1st Lieutenant H. 'George' Schrier, Company E's executive officer, then led a 40-man detachment up the steep path but they came under fire at the top. While some of Schrier's men engaged the Japanese, others found a length of iron pipe and secured a small US flag, measuring no more than 54 inches by 28 inches, to one end; they then raised the Stars and Stripes on the summit of Mount Suribachi. It was 23 February, D+4, the time was 10:20 and Staff Sergeant Lewis Lowery, a journalist for *Leatherneck Magazine*, had caught it all on camera.

Down below, men across the beachhead caught sight of the tiny flag fluttering in the breeze and pointed it out to their comrades. Before long every Marine and Navy man was cheering as they looked towards Suribachi while every vessel in the sea sounded their horns. The flag was an inspiring sight for the thousands of US servicemen on Iwo Jima.

*The second large Stars and Stripes flies proudly above Iwo Jima; now everyone could see it, including the Japanese. These artillery observers are using a high-powered telescope to spot enemy positions. (NARA-127-GW-113721)*

Colonel Liversedge was furious to hear that higher command wanted the flag as a memento and he decided to replace it before it disappeared. Sergeant Michael Strank collected a larger flag (measuring 8 feet by 4 feet 8 inches) from *LST 779* on the beach and carried it to the top followed by Joe Rosenthal, a photographer working for the Associated Press. An impromptu ceremony was organised and Rosenthal took the iconic picture of the second flag raising. His picture was the one that was splashed across every American newspaper over the days that followed and the ceremony has been immortalised by the US Marines memorial in Arlington, Virginia. The flag raising was timed to perfection because Secretary of the Navy, James V. Forrestal and General Holland Smith had just stepped ashore.

The mountain provided a grandstand view of Iwo Jima and the huge fleet off shore and the Marine artillery observers quickly installed their flash-ranging equipment near the summit. The men of RCT 28 did not have time for sightseeing and both 1st and 2nd Battalions spent the afternoon blasting shut cave entrances and hunting down snipers. Many Japanese soldiers were entombed inside the mountain while others committed suicide rather than surrender.

40 men from Company E spent an uneasy night on the summit of Suribachi while the rest of the regiment dug in around the base. Over 120 Japanese tried to escape from the mountain under cover of darkness; they were all killed. Most of them had demolitions

## LAST WORDS

The final message from Mount Suribachi's garrison commander to General Kuribayashi read: 'Enemy's bombardments from the air and sea and their assaults with explosions are very fierce and if we ever try to stay and defend our present positions it will lead us to self-destruction. We should rather like to go out of our position and choose death by banzai charges.'

strapped to their bodies hoping to die gloriously for their Emperor. Another 2000 had had been killed or were buried alive beneath the mountain. 28th Marines had suffered 895 casualties in the five-day battle, 385 of them on the first day.

*Engineers seal the bunkers and caves on Mount Suribachi while the beach below is a hive of activity. (NARA-127-GW-109608)*

## The Battles for Airfield 1 and the Quarry (D+1 to D+2)

To the north the plan was to attack all along V Amphibious Corps' 4000-metre front, following a bombardment by Marine artillery, naval gunfire and air strikes. General Schmidt wanted to complete the pivot north to the O-1 line and while 5th Division advanced along the west coast, 4th Division had to clear Airfield 1's runways and taxiways. Both divisions had to work their way through a fortified zone of bunkers, pillboxes and caves, all camouflaged in the deadly maze of ravines and ridges.

Colonel Wornham's RCT 27 controlled 5th Division's sector, and 1/26th and 3/27th Marines encountered Japanese pillboxes protected by minefields as they moved forward. As they closed in to silence each position, the Japanese mortars and artillery seemed to know exactly when to shoot and where to aim to inflict maximum casualties on the Marines. But with the help

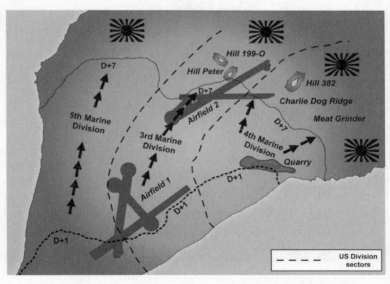

*The advance northeast between D+1 and D+7 (20–26 February).*

of Companies A and B, 5th Tank Battalion, both battalions managed to advance 800 yards.

Two men of 1/26th Marines were awarded the Medal of Honor. Captain Robert H. Dunlap repeatedly crawled forward alone along the cliffs to locate Japanese-held caves. After reporting their location to the artillery and the ships off shore, he risked his life to personally direct their salvoes. Seventeen-year-old Private Jacklyn H. Lucas (he enlisted at the age of fourteen without consent) and three other Marines were ambushed in a narrow ravine. Lucas dived on two grenades when they landed at their feet, absorbing the blast; he was the youngest recipient of the Medal of Honor since the American Civil War. He lived to the age of 80 with more than 200 pieces of shrapnel still in his body.

Colonel Wensinger's RCT 23 had to advance across Airfield 1 on 4th Division's left and both 3/23rd and 2/24th Marines drew heavy fire from every direction as they advanced across the airfield's exposed runway; they both reached the northern perimeter by midday. Anti-tank fire stopped 4th Tank Battalion's Company C crossing the runway, leaving Wensinger's Marines to push on alone beyond the airfield, having overrun an important position held by Colonel Ikeda's 1/145th Battalion.

Colonel Lanigan's RCT 25 had to improve its situation on the ridge overlooking Blue Beach and once 2/25th Marines had captured the high ground in the centre of the regiment's sector, 1/25th Marines could advance alongside RCT 23 on the left. Disaster struck before zero hour when a mortar shell hit 2/25th Battalion's command post wounding several senior officers, including the commanding officers of both the battalion and Company B, 4th Tank Battalion. Lieutenant Colonel Taul, 3/25th Battalion's executive officer, took command and although the attack began on time, the Marines made little progress in the face of heavy crossfire.

RCT 25's bad luck continued when 1/25th Battalion's command post received a direct hit while 1/24th Battalion was hit twice by friendly fire, by an air strike and then an artillery strike and naval

*After spending an anxious night on the beach, these Marines could not wait to be evacuated to one of the hospital ships. (NARA-127-GW-110217)*

gunfire. Despite the problems, Colonel Lanigan was able to report that RCT 25 had pushed its left flank forward by 200 yards.

The build up of supplies continued as the landing craft continued to deliver their cargo to the beach. RCT 25 had to carry their supplies forward by hand from Blue Beach because the LVTs could not reach the front line. All day the Japanese mortars and artillery targeted the beaches and routes inland, hitting supply dumps, evacuation stations and command posts. Shells fell indiscriminately on the congested beaches and wounded men were often hit a second time as they waited to be evacuated.

General Schmidt had ordered Colonel Hartnel J. Withers' RCT 21 to prepare to go ashore but reports concerning the number of broached landing craft, bogged down vehicles and wreckage on the beach made him reconsider his decision. As the wind increased in the early afternoon, so did the surf and RCT 21 had to re-embark and wait for new orders.

General Cates also wanted the rest of his artillery ashore as soon as possible and although 3rd Battalion was launched mid morning it did not go ashore until mid afternoon and it was nightfall before its 105mm howitzers were engaging targets. 4th Battalion was launched into rough water in the afternoon and eight DUKWs floundered and sank, taking over half of the battalion's weapons to the seabed. The survivors did not reach their gun pits until midnight. The first 155mm Howitzer battery belonging to corps artillery came ashore in the afternoon and tractors had to drag them one by one to their firing positions on the west coast.

General Schmidt considered V Amphibious Corps' situation as night fell on 20 February. While progress was being made, casualties were mounting and the beach situation was a growing concern. On the front line, the Marines faced a second disturbed night, as illumination shells and flares lit the sky and gunfire support ships shelled the shore. Yet again the Japanese seemed to be consolidating their positions and they only made two counterattacks; both were stopped in their tracks.

The battle to the northeast began with an early morning barrage of artillery, rockets and naval guns, fired as close to the Marines' positions as the gunners dared. 68 carrier-based planes then hit the area ahead of the Marines' positions.

Along the coast, RCT 27 faced automatic and rifle fire from hidden pillboxes and caves but Colonel Wornham's Marines advanced 1000 yards alongside Sherman tanks towards O-1 line. In 4th Division's sector 23rd and 25th Marines came under heavy fire from positions covering Airfield 2 when they tried to advance. The tanks ran into minefields covered by anti-tank guns and it took the engineers time to crawl forward and clear a route

## CLEARING THE BUNKERS

Sergeant Ross F. Gray, 1/25th Marines, cleared a way through a minefield to reach the emplacements which were pinning down his platoon. He then returned for a satchel charge and used it to destroy the first bunker; he repeated the process until all six bunkers had been silenced. Gray was killed in action six days later. He was awarded the Medal of Honor for his actions.

forward. 23rd Marines advanced 100 metres while 25th Marines advanced less than 50 metres.

In RCT 24's sector, Captain Joseph J. McCarthy's company was pinned down on the edge of Airfield 2 so he gathered together a demolitions and flamethrower team to accompany his rifle squad. They crossed the exposed runway under heavy fire and knocked out two pillboxes on the ridge beyond. McCarthy went on to risk his life several times to save the lives of his men; he was awarded the Medal of Honor. 1/24th Marines advanced the furthest on the right flank, moving 300 yards through the pillboxes and bunkers along the cliffs overlooking East Boat Basin.

General Rockey had left USS *Cecil* (APA 96) in the early afternoon and he set up 5th Division headquarters at the southern end of Airfield 1. Brigadier General Franklin A. Hart, 4th Marine Division's assistant division commander, was already ashore and while he recommended using RCT 21 to relieve RCT 23, it would be impossible to relieve the battered 25th Marines.

The improved weather conditions on D+2 meant that 21st Marines could land on Yellow Beaches during the afternoon and by the evening Colonel Withers' men were in reserve near Airfield 1. However, Blue 1 Beach was under heavy fire and an exploding ammunition dump was endangering everything on Blue and Yellow Beaches. Hart also recommended leaving the division headquarters on board USS *Bayfield* (APA 33) until the following day.

The night of 21/22 February was another one of harassing fire, local counterattacks and infiltration for the Marines. Around midnight 200 enemy troops were spotted advancing from Airfield 2 towards 4th Division, but artillery and naval gun fire dispersed them before they reached the Marines' lines.

The action was not confined to the island on 21 February; around 50 Japanese planes began a three-hour Kamikaze attack against the carrier fleet in the late afternoon. The suicide pilots crashed their planes into three carriers: the *Bismarck Sea* (CVE 95) was sunk; the *Saratoga* (CV 3) was badly damaged and withdrawn; and *Lunga Point* (CVE 94) was hit but continued operations. The *Keokuk* (AKN 4) and *LST 477* were also damaged but the LST was able to land its tanks before withdrawing.

## The Advance towards Airfield 2 and Minami (D+3 and D+4)

Offshore, part of Admiral Spruance's fast carrier force, Task Force 58, left Iwo Jima on 22 February and headed north so it could resume its air strikes against Tokyo. It left behind Task Group 58.5, with the carrier *Enterprise,* the cruisers *Baltimore* and *Flint,* and Destroyer Squadron 54, to provide night fighter protection. The planes on Admiral Durgin's carrier support force would take over close support missions from now on. These planes were based on smaller carriers (CVEs) and they also had to carry out combat air patrols, anti-submarine patrols and searches for crashed aircrew. The change meant that the Marines would sometimes have to go without air support.

Cold, drizzling rain and a driving wind soaked the Marines to the skin on D+3 while the wet volcanic ash clogged up their weapons and clung to their boots. The advance towards the O-1 Line had been slower than anticipated while casualties had been higher. Fatigue was becoming a problem after three days in action and both Generals Rockey and Cates were anxious to relieve some of their front line units so they could rest and absorb replacements.

*While the rest of 4th Division cleared Airstrip 1, 24th Marines fought their way onto the high ground above the Quarry, losing over 100 men; many of them from friendly fire. There are anxious faces all along the front as zero hour approaches. (NARA-127-GW-111245)*

Colonel Grahams' RCT 26 relieved RCT 27 in 5th Division's sector but a combination of bad luck, rain and heavy resistance meant that 3rd Battalion could not advance on the right flank. Both Lieutenant Colonel Trotti and the operations officer, Major Day, were killed, leaving a company commander in charge. Although 2nd Battalion advanced 400 yards along the coast by nightfall it had to withdraw to maintain contact with 3rd Battalion.

On 4th Division's left flank, RCT 21 (attached from 3rd Division) took all morning to relieve RCT 23 and Colonel Withers' Marines then found a maze of pillboxes covering Airfield 2 waiting for them. Tanks were unable to cross the rough terrain and Marines edged alone up the rocky slopes towards them. While heavy rain blinded both the carrier planes and the Marine artillery observers, the Japanese artillery and mortar crews continued firing on registered targets.

On 4th Division's right flank, RCT 25 was hoping that its 1st Battalion would reach the O-1 Line. While Major Mee's men advanced 200 yards, they had to withdraw due to RCT 21's lack of progress on its flank. A rocket attack in 3rd Battalion's sector flushed 200 Japanese soldiers out into the open and the Marines cut them down with their machine guns. It was one of the largest groups of enemy soldiers seen together on Iwo Jima.

The rain and mist continued into the night, and the Japanese took advantage of the conditions to make two counterattacks. After midnight, a group of Japanese swam ashore on the western beaches and infiltrated 27th Marines' camp in 5th Division's reserve. It took until dawn to hunt them all down. Around 100 Japanese also infiltrated 4th Division's sector.

On 23 February RCT 26 was supposed to take the bluffs that dominated 5th Division's sector on the western side of the island. Colonel Graham's men could then fire onto the Japanese positions protecting Airfield 2 in 4th Division's sector and he had permission to cross the divisional boundary if necessary. However, it was the Japanese around Airfield 2 who brought RCT 26 under heavy enfilade fire and General Rockey had to report that his Marines had made no progress. The fact that all his armour was re-equipping and reorganising had not helped.

On 4th Division's left, RCT 21's attack across Airfield 2 was doomed without supporting fire from RCT 26 and Colonel Withers' eventually ordered his men to dig in along the southern perimeter of the runway. Corporal Hershel W. Williams began the day by escorting the tanks through a network of pillboxes. He then went on to spray each one with his flamethrower while his riflemen used demolition charges to knock them out. Williams was awarded the Medal of Honor for his part in RCT 21's advance.

On 4th Division's right, RCT 24 relieved RCT 25 and had advanced 300 yards before it was ordered to stop due to the holdup in RCT 21's sector. The problem for V Amphibious Corps was that a delay in one sector had a knock-on effect on both flanks. The advance had to be even all along the line to stop gaps opening up, gaps that the Japanese would infiltrate.

While the battle raged around Airfield 2, the logistics operations along the beach were starting to become organised. D+3 had been a difficult day due to the poor weather and the rough surf stopped small craft and amphibious vehicles collecting the wounded. LST 807 had unloaded its supplies and the decision was taken to leave it on the beach as a temporary hospital ship; over 200 injured men were treated on the ship during the night. The calmer weather on D+4 meant that unloading could begin in earnest as the LSMs rushed vital supplies from the cargo ships to the shore, including 2500 rounds of badly needed 81mm ammunition. 25 tanks of Major Holly H. Evans' 3rd Tank Battalion also landed. While the Japanese artillery fire on the beach had diminished, the routes

*Lieutenant Michael F. Keleher, a battalion surgeon, described Blue Beach: 'Wrecked boats, bogged-down jeeps, tractors and tanks; burning vehicles; casualties scattered all over.' (NARA-127-GW-109604)*

off the beach were being improved. All these factors allowed the shore parties to tidy up the chaos. However, the weather forecast predicted a shift in the wind direction over the next 48 hours making the surf too rough to land on the eastern beaches. The Attack Force Commander ordered V Amphibious Corps to prepare the western beaches for unloading and the corps engineers spent all day preparing them for the shore parties.

General Cates had left USS *Bayfield* on the morning of 23 February and opened 4th Division's advance command post east of Airfield Number 1. With both the 4th and 5th Division commanders ashore, General Schmidt landed and discussed plans for renewing the attack in the morning.

## Clearing Airfield 2 and the Advance to Charlie-Dog Ridge (D+5 to D+7)

The attack on 24 February opened with a naval bombardment of the Japanese positions covering Airfield 2. The corps artillery then joined in and finally the carrier planes flew over, carpeting the area with bombs and rockets. 5th Division had to hold its ground until 4th Division had cleared the ridge running between them and General Cates had placed it at the top of his priorities.

RCT 21's armoured support ran into trouble on the taxiways connecting Airfield 1 to Airfield 2. Half the tanks were delayed by mines on the western taxiway and then stopped by anti-tank guns; after five had been knocked out, the rest withdrew. The other half had to wait until a route had been cleared through the minefield on the eastern taxiway. Eventually twelve tanks joined RCT 21 and by midday 3/21st Marines had crossed the runway and reached the high ground on the far side. Three times the Marines cleared the summit at bayonet point but each time they were driven off by Japanese artillery fire.

3rd Battalion persevered and Colonel Withers was pleased to report that his Marines had control of the runways having advanced nearly 800 yards. Tanks then accompanied 2nd Battalion onto the

*Tanks often struggled to get across the tortuous terrain to help the Marines, but once they did the Japanese often withdrew. This Sherman, nicknamed* Bed Bug, *crawls forward past a grim faced group of Marines as they wait for the order to advance. (NARA-127-GW-109666)*

runway but only one company could get across. At the same time RCT 26 in 5th Division's sector was making good progress west of Airfield 2. In fact it was advancing too fast and its 3rd Battalion had to withdraw due to enfilade fire from 3rd Division's sector.

In 4th Division's sector, 2/24th Marines advanced quickly until it came under fire from Charlie-Dog Ridge at the eastern end of Airfield 2's runway. Machine guns, snipers and anti-tank guns forced the Marines to look for cover and then the Japanese mortars and artillery zeroed in. Air and naval support were refused because the Marines were too close to the Japanese positions, so they had to drag four machine guns and a 37mm gun forward. Once they were in position, G Company renewed its advance, burning and blasting its way to the top of the ridge. When Company I had done the same, Company F advanced to Airfield 2's runway making contact with RCT 21.

The southeast extension of Charlie-Dog Ridge was known as the Amphitheatre and the Japanese had a perfect field of fire over

*Officer casualties were heavy but the survivors rallied their men and led them towards their objectives. Two company commanders discuss how to coordinate their covering fire. (NARA-127-GW-111107)*

RCT 24's line of advance. 3rd Battalion was hit by a devastating crossfire as it moved forward while the Japanese artillery and mortars knew exactly where to fire. The Marines were soon pinned down and the battalion's mortars had to fire white phosphorous smoke to shield the medics while they evacuated the casualties; even the commanding officer, Lieutenant Colonel Vandegrift Jr was wounded.

Meanwhile, 1st Battalion advanced 500 yards through the maze of ravines and caves along the coast, and although they were always under fire, they rarely saw the enemy. A report to the Japanese Naval Headquarters reported the bizarre battle RCT 24 was fighting. 'At the present time there is the unusual situation in the southern sector area of our troops all being underground, while the enemy troops are above ground.'

During the morning General Schmidt left USS *Auburn* and came ashore to assume command of the battle. Although 4th Division had been unable to make any progress on the right, the salient in the centre of V Amphibious Corps' centre had been eliminated where 3rd Division had made significant progress across Airfield 2. He found all manner of command posts, artillery positions, supply dumps and medical installations in the shadow of Mount Suribachi. 3rd Division's command post only added to the congestion but General Erskine needed to be ashore to command the battle around Airfield 2. The rest of 3rd Division was coming ashore across Red 2 and Yellow 1 Beaches, an area renamed Black Beach. Rough surf conditions meant that LCMs were being used to transfer everything from ship to shore and it took all day to get 9th Marines and 3rd Tank Battalion ashore; 3rd Division's artillery, 12th Marines could only land a battery of 75mm pack howitzers.

3rd Division took over Airfield 2 on 25 February and RCT 21 reverted to its control. General Graves B. Erskine had orders to advance beyond the airfield and across the Motoyama Plateau to Airfield 3. While the plateau was relatively flat, the Japanese had fortified it with bunkers, pillboxes, minefields and tank ditches. Observers on the hills either side of 3rd Division's sector would also be able to bring down mortar and artillery fire where needed.

While RCT 9 passed through RCT 21, a battleship and two cruisers targeted the Japanese positions facing 3rd Division. Then the corps artillery shelled the area north of Airfield 2 followed by airstrikes. Even so, 1st Battalion suffered many casualties as it crossed Airfield 2's runway and the high ground beyond. 2nd Battalion could not advance along the low ridge on the west side of the airfield and nine of the 26 tanks supporting its attack were knocked out. Colonel Howard N. Kenyon had to take the ridge to safeguard 1st Battalion's position so 3rd Battalion was released from reserve to help 2nd Battalion. It too became pinned down and fell back in confusion after two company commanders were killed. It took until nightfall to stabilise the situation but 2nd Battalion was finally established on the all-important ridge.

V Amphibious Corps hit the Amphitheatre and Minami areas in front of 4th Division with all the artillery, naval gunfire and carrier planes it could muster. LVT(A)s from Company A, 2nd Armored

*A young Marine waits for orders to move out. He still has scraps of waterproofing attached to the end of his rifle. (NARA-127-GW-112202)*

Amphibian Battalion also tried to give support from the sea but the choppy conditions meant they had to withdraw.

3/23rd Marines had taken over the eastern end of Airfield 2 on the morning of 25 February and it had to advance alone onto Charlie-Dog Ridge while the engineers cleared a route for its armoured support. Tanks could not reach RCT 24 either and 1st and 2nd Battalions only advanced 100 yards towards the Amphitheatre.

By D+6 General Schmidt was aware that the landing craft and ships had to be withdrawn soon so they could be prepared for the invasion of Okinawa. The beaches had to be cleared so they could be unloaded as quickly as possible, with ammunition being the number one priority. The eastern beaches were not enough, especially if the wind changed to an easterly direction, and the rest of the western beaches had to be developed. (The western beaches would eventually be codenamed as follows from north to south: Orange 1 and 2, White 1 and 2, Brown 1 and 2 and Purple.) It meant that 5th Division had to clear the Japanese from the high ground overlooking them.

5th Division had to advance on 26 February even though the ridge on its right was still in Japanese hands. While 2/27th Battalion advanced 400 yards along the coast, it was the division's only success. The rest of RCT 26 was hit by crossfire from camouflaged bunkers to their front and hidden guns on the ridge to their flank. Neither 2nd nor 3rd Battalions had moved far when low cloud obscured the island, making it impossible for the artillery or the tanks

*Colonel Pollock receives his new orders at 1/26 Marines makeshift headquarters while runners lie in the sand, waiting to pass on the message. (NARA-127-GW-112670)*

to spot targets. There was still 900 yards to go to 5th Division's next objective – the high ground around Hill 362A – and the Japanese could watch the Marines every move from the summit.

RCT 9's attack in 3rd Division's sector was a disaster and the only good news that Colonel Kenyon heard was that a flame tank had reached the far side of Hill Peter and burned out the escape tunnel. In 4th Division's area, RCT 23 came under devastating fire on the slopes of Hill 382 but while 1st Battalion could not advance, 3rd Battalion could, owing to Private First Class Douglas T. Jacobson's one-man crusade. After knocking out an anti-aircraft gun with his bazooka, he advanced towards the summit of Hill 382, destroying two machine-gun positions and two pillboxes. He then cleared a line of seven earth-covered rifle emplacements so that the rest of his platoon could get to the main one. Jacobson then joined another company, knocking out two pillboxes and a tank with his bazooka. He was awarded the Medal of Honor for destroying 16 enemy positions and killing around 75 Japanese.

The Japanese were not going to give up the hill without a fight; 'The enemy was determined to deny us Hill 382, and his unusually heavy mortar barrage on it twice forced our troops to retire after having occupied the hill area.' Both battalions had to postpone their attempts to take the hill until the following day and dug in close to the summit.

## DEATH AT CLOSE QUARTERS

25th Marines noticed that the 'the enemy was now fighting to the death in pillboxes, foxholes and trenches in its area and is not retreating as he apparently formerly had done.' The close proximity of the front lines meant that the artillery, the ships and the carrier planes could no longer give any assistance and to make matters worse, the tanks could not move through the rough terrain. The Marines had to fight on alone.

# SECURING
# THE ISLAND
# (D+8 TO D+19)

On 28 February the engineers announced that Airfield 1 was open for business. It meant that the carrier-based planes could transfer ashore and continue to observe for the Marines' artillery and hunt for Japanese battery positions. Their presence in the skies was enough to stop many guns crews firing, in case they were spotted. The first plane landed without any problems but the second plane was lost overboard before it could be launched. Ten more observation planes would transfer to Airfield 1 over the next two days.

By now V Amphibious Corps had all of its three divisions in line and they could not ease up the pressure, they had to keep attacking. 5th Division faced a difficult advance along the north coast towards Hill 362-A while 3rd Division had to take Hill 199-O and Hill Peter before advancing towards Airfield 3; 4th Division faced the area known as the 'Meat Grinder'. We shall consider each division in turn over the next seven days of the bloody battle to break the Japanese resistance on Iwo Jima.

## 5th Division's Advance to Hill 362A and Nishi Ridge (D+8 to D+14)

RCT 27 took over from RCT 26 on 27 February and Colonel Wornham had instructions to take Hill 362-A, an area of high

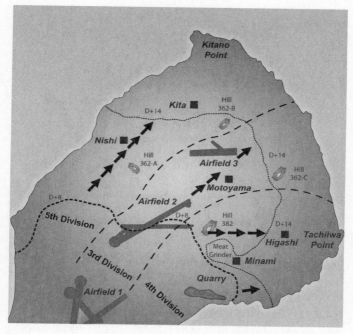

*The advance northeast between D+8 and D+14 (27 February–5 March).*

ground dominating the north side of the island. 2nd Battalion made slow but steady progress along the beach and cliff tops and by nightfall it had advanced 500 metres, straightening out the division's front line.

The rest of RCT 27 ran into heavy opposition and while a nest of pillboxes stopped 1st Battalion after only 200 metres, 3rd Battalion struggled to advance because the tanks could not climb Hill 362A's rocky slopes. Heavy machine-gun fire forced a halftrack armed with a 75mm gun to withdraw, leaving the Marines to tackle each bunker alone.

V Corps designated a new objective line for 5th Division on 28 February. The O-3 line would place General Rockey's Marines across the northern side of the Motoyama plateau, overlooking the sea. However, there was a long way to go as RCT 27 was still

## THE GREATEST SACRIFICE

Gunnery Sergeant William G. Walsh's platoon had been forced to fall back down a steep slope under heavy fire during 2/27th Marines' attack but it regrouped and he led it back up to the summit despite being outnumbered. One group of Japanese made a last stand, showering Walsh's platoon with grenades and when one landed in their trench, he dived to the ground and absorbed the force of the explosion. Walsh was posthumously awarded the Medal of Honor.

300 metres from the top of Hill 362A. 3rd Battalion managed to reach the foot of the hill and by the afternoon patrols were looking for a way up to the fortified summit. During the advance, Corpsman John H. Willis administered first aid to many Marines until he too was wounded but did not wait to be discharged from the aid post and returned to his company. After hearing about a man injured in No Man's Land he crawled out and dragged him to the safety of a shellhole. While Willis administering blood plasma, the Japanese threw grenades at him; he threw back eight but the ninth exploded in his hand and killed him; he was posthumously awarded the Medal of Honor.

1st Battalion was also advancing onto the ridge south of Hill 362A aided by tanks when the Japanese counterattacked in the late afternoon. Although RCT 27 eventually stopped the attack, both of Colonel Wornham's battalions had to withdraw; it was a disappointing end to a promising day.

RCT 28 cleared the summit of Hill 362A on 1 March and advanced into the valley beyond only to find another line of fortifications waiting for them along Nishi Ridge. Colonel Liversedge's Marines were crossing the valley, split for most part by a steep-sided rocky ravine, to get to them, when they came under heavy fire from machine guns, snipers and mortars. 1st Battalion

*With bayonet fixed, a Marine risks sniper fire to call out mortar hits on his platoon, hoping to locate the Japanese position for the artillery. (NARA-127-GW-109954)*

tried to outflank the death trap to bring the ridge under fire but found it impossible to advance. Only 3rd Battalion could advance on the left flank and it did so until it was ordered to stop and tie in with the rest of the regiment.

On 2 March General Schmidt ordered General Rockey to make his main effort on the right to keep in contact with 3rd Division on the Motoyama Plateau. Although he had designated half the corps' artillery to support RCT 26, the Japanese soldiers kept close to the Marines' lines to avoid the barrage. The area was a mass of broken rocks and although there were few bunkers in the area, at times it seemed that there was a Japanese soldier hiding behind every rock and in every crevice. Even so, 3rd Battalion advanced on to the eastern end of Nishi Ridge, and Colonel Graham ordered the rest of the regiment forward to cover its flanks.

## SUPPORT FROM THE SEA

Large support landing craft used their 40mm guns to target the caves and ravines on the west coast in support of 5th Division's advance. The observers became experts at distinguishing between friendly and enemy troops and the division placed its own observer teams aboard on 28 February. The landing craft played a valuable role in stopping Japanese attempts to reach the supply dumps on the western beaches.

In RCT 28's zone to the west, 1st and 2nd Battalions put suppressive fire on Nishi Ridge while a tank dozer and an armoured bulldozer made a road across an anti-tank ditch. Once 5th Battalion's tanks could get forward, so could the Marines, and they worked closely together as they inched up the slopes of Nishi Ridge. Colonel Liversedge was delighted to hear that 1st and 2nd Battalions reached the crest and even more so when they stopped the Japanese retaking it in the afternoon. RCT 28 now had a foothold on the high ground overlooking the north end of the island. 3rd Battalion had also edged forward along the rugged coastline, clearing over 60 caves.

5th Division held an uneven line by nightfall on 2 March but the morning attack soon evened it out when all three battalions moved into extremely rugged terrain. It was later described by the division intelligence officer:

Volcanic eruption has littered the whole northern end of the island with outcrops of sandstone and loose rock. The sandstone outcrops made cave digging easy for the Japs ... Our troops obtained cover only by defilade or by piling loose rocks on the surface to form rock-revetted positions. A series of irregularly eroded, crisscrossed gorges with precipitous sides resulted in a series of compartments of various shapes. These were usually small but some extended for several hundred metres. The compartments were lined with a labyrinth of natural and artificial caves which covered the approaches from all directions. Fields of fire were usually limited to 25 metres and a unique or at least unusual characteristic of the Japanese defensive positions in this area was that the reverse slopes were as strongly fortified as were the forward slopes.

The fighting was at close quarters so neither the artillery, navy nor aircraft could not help and General Rockey's Marines had to work alongside tanks and half-tracks or manhandle 37mm guns forward. All companies suffered heavy casualties in the rocky maze but they kept advancing and news that 2/26th Marines had reached the summit of Hill 362B in the late afternoon was welcomed by all.

Three men of 26th Marines were awarded the Medal of Honor for deeds performed on 3 March. Platoon corpsman George E.

*Marines have manhandled this howitzer into rough terrain where tanks could not travel so they could fire directly at a Japanese bunker. (NARA-127-GW-113644)*

Wahlen had risked his life several times on 26 February to save the men in his platoon despite his own injuries, even treating casualties of another platoon. He did the same during 2nd Battalion's advance on 2 and 3 March, again ignoring his own injuries to save others.

Private First Class William R. Caddy of 3rd Battalion was advancing with his platoon leader and another Marine when a sniper forced them to find shelter in a shellhole. During the fight that followed a grenade landed amongst them and Caddy threw himself upon it; he was posthumously awarded the Medal of Honor.

During the night hours, Japanese soldiers launched a surprise attack against 1st Battalion and when a grenade fell into Corporal Charles J. Berry's foxhole he dived on the missile to save his comrades; he was also posthumously awarded the Medal of Honor for his sacrifice.

Two men of 28th Marines were also awarded the Medal of Honor. Platoon corpsman Jack Williams went in front of 3rd Battalion's lines to rescue a wounded Marine under fire. After dragging him into a shallow depression he administered first aid, screening the injured man with his body. He was hit three times but completed his work before dressing his own wounds. Williams was killed by a sniper while heading back after assisting another wounded man.

Later that evening Sergeant William G. Harrell was guarding a company command post when the Japanese infiltrated 1st Battalion's lines. He fought a number of soldiers for several hours, losing both hands and suffering a fractured thigh in the vicious battle. Almost incredibly, an exhausted and bleeding Harrell was found the following morning surrounded by dead Japanese; he was evacuated.

After eight days of favourable weather it changed for the worse on 4 March. Overcast skies and showers forced air strikes to be cancelled while artillery and mortar observers struggled to spot targets. It left the Marines to edge forward slowly with the tanks and engineers.

# 3rd Division's Advance to Motoyama and Airfield 3 (D+8 and D+14)

On 27 February RCT 9 cleared the high ground northeast of Airfield 2 and while 2nd Battalion inched up the slopes of Hill 199 Oboe, 1st Battalion reached the summit of Hill Peter. The Japanese had dug into the reverse slope and although Colonel Kenyon's Marines came under fire as they moved over the crest, both battalions kept advancing. By the end of the day they had cleared the hills. Colonel Kenyon proudly wrote of his men's achievements:

Features of this action were the skill, determination, and aggressiveness displayed by our own troops; the unprecedented tenacity and defensive resourcefulness displayed by the enemy ... the decisive aid rendered infantry troops by tanks; and finally, the excellent coordination of all supporting units with infantry maneuvers.

A Marine hugs the ground during RCT 21's drive towards Airfield 2. (NARA-127-GW-111389)

The capture of Hill 199 Oboe was accelerated by one man: Private D. Watson. After his squad was pinned down he rushed the pillbox, firing into the embrasure before hurling a grenade inside; he then gunned down the survivors as they ran out. When his squad was pinned down a second time, he climbed the slope with his assistant and charged into the heart of the Japanese position, standing over the entrenchments, shooting anyone that moved. By the time the rest of his platoon reached Watson, he had killed around 60 Japanese; he was awarded the Medal of Honor.

V Corps designated a new O-3 line on 28 February and 3rd Division's objective was to clear the centre of Motoyama plateau, including the unfinished Airfield 3. RCT 21 took over the attack and while 1st Battalion was stopped by a strongpoint on Hill 362-A's eastern slopes, 3rd Battalion advanced 400 metres towards Motoyama village. A gap was opening in the centre of RCT 21 but 2nd Battalion was unable to move through it to outflank the strong point in front of 1st Battalion. Despite the disappointment at not reaching Airfield 3, General Erskine was able to report that 3rd Division was through the centre of the Japanese main line of resistance.

RCT 21 again tried to capture Airfield 3 on 1 March but a gap opened up in the centre of 2nd and 3rd Battalions' advance. 3/9th Marines was ordered forward and it crossed the west end of the

## MOVING FAST

General Erskine and his regimental commanders were always looking for a weak spot in the Japanese defences to exploit. They probed them as far as they dared, using reserves to protect open flanks, and then widened the gaps by launching attacks from the sides of the openings. These daring tactics speeded up the rate of advance but the Marines had to watch out for overlooked bunkers and pillboxes during the mopping up process.

airfield's runway before outflanking the Japanese position that had been holding up 1/21st Marines all day. A second attempt to advance in the afternoon made no further progress.

Hill 362B overlooked RCT 21's line of advance and General Erskine obtained permission to cross the division boundary to attack it on 2 March. But first RCT 9 had to seize Airfield 3 so it could give RCT 21 covering fire on Hill 362B. Unfortunately, RCT 9 failed to the cross the runway and Colonel Kenyon had to be satisfied with holding the southern perimeter of the runway while a platoon of tanks moved up to give covering fire. While 1/21st Battalion advanced around the north side of the runway and 3/9th Battalion seized the high ground at the east end, 2/21st Battalion reinforce the airfield perimeter in case the Japanese decided to counterattack across the runway.

The battle for Airfield 3 continued on 3 March but while RCT 9 could make no progress, RCT 21 had seized Hill 357 by mid morning. The summit gave Major George A. Percy's Marines an uninterrupted view of the east coast and there appeared to be no organised resistance between them and the sea. Colonel Withers was then ordered to turn southeast to outflank the Japanese positions in front of RCT 9. While 1st Battalion moved forward along the runway's northern perimeter there was now a gap in the centre of the division. Shortly after midnight 200 Japanese crept across the runway hoping to infiltrate 3rd Division's lines; they were soon stopped.

4 March was a miserable day for the 3rd Division and the promises of a breakthrough the previous day were soon dashed. RCT 21 struggled to make any progress east of Airfield 3 while RCT 9 failed to get any closer to Hill 362-C. Both men and units were reaching the limits of their endurance and V Amphibious Corps had ordered 5 March to be a day of rest – or rather reorganisation in the morning and resupply in the afternoon – ready for an attack the following morning. While the Marines checked their equipment and distributed supplies, the tanks and bulldozers withdrew for some overdue maintenance.

*A young Marine watches intently for signs of life as he moves towards a Japanese bunker. (NARA-127-GW-112862)*

## 4th Division in the Meat Grinder (D+8 and D+14)

4th Division faced the rugged area around the ruins of Minami village on 27 February. The area was criss-crossed by crevices and ridges but the main geographical features were known as Hill 382 (or *Nidan Iwa*), the Turkey Knob and the Amphitheatre; collectively they would become known as the Meat Grinder.

The Japanese had dug camouflaged emplacements into the slopes of Hill 382 and hidden tanks and artillery pieces in its crevices and ravines, linking many positions with a network of tunnels. They had also fortified the hollowed-out summit with

*Marines of RCT 9 watch as P-51 Mustangs fly low to drop their 1000lb bombs on Japanese fortifications. (NARA-127-GW-178526)*

artillery pieces and anti-tank guns. The huge rocky outcrop known as the Turkey Knob had a concrete communication post on the summit and Japanese observers had an uninterrupted view across the Meat Grinder. The Marines had to cross open ground to reach the only access to the summit and it was overlooked by a ridge – the Amphitheatre. The Japanese had built three tiers of concrete emplacements on the south-sloping hillside and they would have a grandstand view of the Marines' every move. An intelligence report summarises the hell General Cates' Marines faced:

> The volcanic, crevice-lined area is a tangled conglomeration of torn trees and blasted rocks. Ground observation is restricted to small areas. While there are sundry ridges, depressions and irregularities, most of the crevices of any moment radiate from the direction of Hill 382 to fan out like spokes generally in a south easterly direction providing a series of cross corridors to our advance and eminently suitable for the enemy's employment of mortars. The general debris caused by our supporting fire

provides perfect concealment for snipers and mortar positions. From the air, caves and tracks are observed everywhere, but the enemy's camouflage discipline is flawless and it is the rarest occasion that an Aerial Observer can locate troops.

On 27 February RCT 23 faced Hill 382 on 4th Division's left flank but its 3rd Battalion had to capture a ruined radar station before it could begin its ascent. The Marines struggled to advance until tanks reached the front line in the afternoon but even then artillery and mortar fire stopped them from taking the summit. RCT 23 made good progress on 28 February and while 1st Battalion moved across the hill's northern slopes, 2nd Battalion advanced along a ravine to the south. By the end of the day Colonel Wensinger was pleased to report that his Marines had nearly surrounded the hill.

On 27 February RCT 25 faced the Turkey Knob in 4th Division's centre and Colonel Lanigan planned to surround the rocky outcrop and then look for ways to reach the hilltop bunker. 3rd Battalion advanced 200 metres on the right but 2nd Battalion hardly made any progress up the slopes of the Amphitheatre in the centre. 1st Battalion's advance on the left was delayed until the afternoon but it did not go far after hidden anti-tank guns knocked out three tanks.

## ROCKET MEN

The rocket trucks of the 1st Provisional Rocket Detachment were able to deliver a devastating barrage of 4.5-inch rockets against a Japanese strongpoint. However, they were easy to spot and vulnerable to counter-battery fire. Each section of six trucks became adapt at driving into position, firing two salvoes, and withdrawing to safety before the Japanese artillery could retaliate. It took less than five minutes to fire a total of 432 rockets.

RCT 25 repeated its attempt to surround the Turkey Knob on 28 February, only this time 1st Battalion tried to advance around both sides of the outcrop. The left hook was stopped by a camouflaged nest of bunkers and while reinforcements moved up, the right hook attacked; it too was stopped in its tracks. Neither 2nd nor 3rd Battalion could help out and mortars had to smother the Turkey Knob with smoke while 1st Battalion withdrew to safety.

In the early hours of 1 March a shell hit 4th Division's ammunition dump, filling the night sky with explosions. It took five hours to douse the fires, by which time 20 per cent of the division's supply of ammunition was lost. Another shell had also disabled V Corps artillery fire direction centre.

RCT 24 relieved RCT 23 on 1 March and while Colonel Jordan had orders to clear Hill 382, his attack was delayed for three hours waiting for artillery support. Although all three battalions advanced, they were stopped by heavy fire on the reverse slopes and the summit remained in Japanese hands.

*As the battle grew to a climax and the surviving Japanese troops were pushed into a corner, the fighting became more desperate. Marines hug the rocks as a demolition charge explodes in a mass of flames and smoke. (NARA-127-GW-114292)*

Tanks and rocket launchers plastered Hill 382 until they had to withdraw and then the Marines moved in. Major Frank E. Garretson, 2nd Battalion's executive officer, later explained the means that had to be used to clear the hill. 'Artillery and naval gunfire was paving the way out in front, but the resistance close in had to be dealt with as usual by the attacking companies employing hand grenades, rifles, and automatic rifles, 60mm mortars, flamethrowers, demolitions, and bazookas.' On the afternoon of 2 March Colonel Jordan finally reported that Hill 382 had been taken.

The poor weather on 4 March affected General Cates' plans the same as the rest. While airstrikes had to be cancelled, artillery observers found it difficult to find targets. The Marines would have noticed that the amount of Japanese artillery fire had fallen since the fall of Hill 382 and its accuracy had noticeably worsened. Instead Japanese soldiers were hiding in camouflaged positions until the Marines were so close that they could not use their support weapons. Attempts to advance down the reverse slopes towards Higashi over the next 48 hours came to nothing; RCT 24 was exhausted.

RCT 25 renewed the pincer attack on the Turkey Knob on 1 March but yet again 1st Battalion's hooks were unable to surround the outcrop and mortars created a smoke screen so the Marines could gather up their casualties and withdraw to safety. Colonel

## A LENGTHY, DEADLY PROCESS

It took several days to clear all the bunkers and caves on Hill 382; 4th Division's operations officer described RCT 24's mopping up operation:
'It appears that there are underground passageways leading into the defences on Hill 382 and when an occupant of a pillbox is killed another one comes up to take his place. This is a rather lengthy process.'.

Lanigan chose to make a surprise attack on 2 March and 1st Battalion moved out before dawn, creeping forward round the north side of the Turkey Knob for 20 minutes before they were spotted. Then all hell was let loose and the Marines had to fight for their lives until eight tanks could reach them. They fired hundreds of 75mm shells and squirted over 1000 gallons of flamethrower fuel at the blockhouse but the garrison refused to abandon their hilltop position. As night fell Colonel Lanigan had to yet again recall his men to safer positions.

Two battalions tried to sneak past the Turkey Knob early on 3 March and while 2/24th Battalion closed in from the northeast, 1/23rd Battalion crept past the Amphitheatre until it was spotted. The Marines had to wait behind cover until engineers cleared a route forward for a flame tank, and as it smothered the blockhouse in burning liquid, 1/23rd Battalion continued their advance. The story was the same on 4 March: heavy casualties

*Soft sand and rough terrain limited where tanks could operate. The leading tank has become bogged down in a huge crater; the second has lost a track. (NARA-127-GW-111039)*

*On 4 March the first B-29 Superfortress,* Dinah Might, *landed on Iwo Jima so it could carry out emergency repairs as it returned from a raid over Tokyo. The sight of the huge plane taking off and heading for its home base gave the Marines a morale boost. (NARA-127-GW-112392)*

and a small advance because RCT 23 was also exhausted. Late in the afternoon General Schmidt issued orders instructing all divisions to dig in for the night; after 14 days of constant battling, the Marines needed a well-deserved rest.

By this stage of the battle many companies were at half strength or less and battalion commanders had to transfer men between companies to keep them in action while the headquarters and support weapons companies were ordered to send men forward to the rifle companies. Companies, platoons and squads had lost too many leaders, and it took time to integrate the replacements with the veterans. 26th Marines, for example, had its original strength of 3256 reduced to 2153 effectives; 464 were newcomers. Colonel Graham could only rate his regiment's combat efficiency at less than 50 per cent and it was the same situation across all three divisions.

The day of rest allowed time for new plans to be made. Two weeks of sustained bombardment had altered Iwo Jima's terrain beyond all recognition, rendering many operational maps worthless. A public relations photographer was ordered to carry out an improvised aerial photography mission to try and restore the situation. He took many photographs of the island and after they had been developed and enlarged they were distributed to the divisions. Intelligence officers in turn studied them to gain a better understanding of the terrain.

## 5th Division's Advance to Kitano Ravine (D+15 to D+19)

5th Division wanted to clear Hill 362-B on its right flank on 6 March but 2/27th Marines was hit by a counter barrage at zero hour and never recovered. 1/26th and 3/26th Marines extended the attack across 5th Division's sector in the afternoon but to no avail. 5th Division had to ask for help from carrier planes: 'Request close support planes be armed maximum amount napalm for duration operation. Urgent need in ravines along northeast coast...' It appeared that the Japanese only feared fire.

By 7 March, ammunition expenditure was outstripping supply and everyone agreed that artillery barrages were having little effect on the Japanese troops. Corps and division artillery were ordered to reduce the number of firing missions while V Amphibious Corps insisted on something different: pre-dawn surprise attacks. Recent experience in 4th Division's zone had shown that progress could be made by creeping across the rugged terrain in complete silence. The plan was for them to be deep into the Japanese lines before they were spotted. Then the Marines faced a fight for survival until the tanks could get forward.

RCT 26 advanced 200 metres beyond Kita before dawn on 7 March, bypassing several strongpoints before they were spotted. Colonel Graham's Marines then had to fight for their lives to hold the ground they had taken. Meanwhile, RCT 28 continued to inch forward along the rocky, gorge-cut north coast. On the right flank 2/27th Marines were pinned down in a steep-sided gully

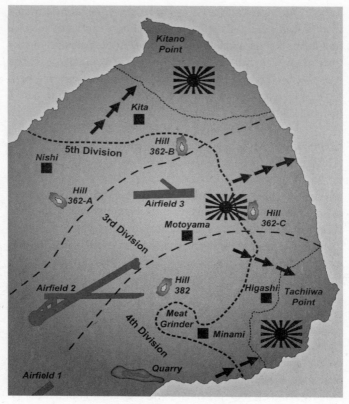

*The drive for the east coast, D+15 and D+19 (6–10 March).*

beyond Hill 362-B and as tanks could not reach them, the Marines manhandled a 37mm gun forward; it was unable to make a difference and they had to withdraw.

On 8 March General Rockey received V Amphibious Corps's new order, an order issued to all three divisions: 'capture the remainder of the island.' As RCT 28 advanced another 400 metres along the north coast, ships fired into the caves and ravines ahead of the Marines. It was a different story for RCT 26; they were unable to make progress through the maze of pillboxes

5th Division had to clear out dozens of caves along the rugged northern coastline. Flamethrowers were used to kill or injure anyone inside and then the engineers moved in with their explosives. (NARA-111-SC-208586)

and caves around Kita. 2/27th Battalion was also struggling to advance until Lieutenant Jack Lummus, a popular officer who played for the New York Giants football team before the war, was mortally wounded. Lummus had single-handedly made the hard yards, knocking out the two strongpoints stopping his platoon and encouraging his men to advance while directing tanks forward. After knocking out a third emplacement Lummus was fatally wounded by a land mine and it was all too much for Company E. Lummus's men rushed forward in a surge of fury, making the 300-yard dash to the cliff top overlooking the sea. Lummus had been a constant inspiration to his men since D-Day and his death was just too much; he was posthumously awarded the Medal of Honor.

On 5th Division's left flank, RCT 28 also continued its coastal advance until it came to the edge of a deep gorge known as Kitano Ravine. Colonel Liversedge was advised not to send his Marines down to investigate until it had been surrounded because it was believed that General Kuribayashi and 109th

## An Honourable Death

During the night of on 8 March, Private First Class James D. La Belle of 27th Marines' Weapons Company was on watch in his foxhole when a grenade landed close by. With no time to pick it up, he shouted a warning to his two buddies and dived on the missile; he was posthumously awarded the Medal of Honor.

Division headquarters were in the maze of caves below. They had possibly been joined by part of 2nd Battalion, 145th Regiment and 3rd Battalion, 17th Independent Mixed Regiment. A large number of stragglers had also made their way into the narrow gorge.

RCT 26 and RCT 27 Marines continued to edge forward on 9 March, pushing the Japanese defenders towards Kitano Point but many chose to fight to the death or commit suicide because they had nowhere to hide. When 1/27th Battalion came under enfilade fire, Sergeant Joseph R. Julian ordered his machine guns to return fire while he rushed the pillbox and knocked it out with a satchel charge and white phosphorus grenades; he then grabbed a discarded rifle and killed the escaping soldiers. Julian went on to silence two more cave positions with another Marine and was mortally wounded while trying to knock out another pillbox with a bazooka; he was posthumously awarded the Medal of Honor.

Between 25 February and 10 March, 5th Division had advanced 3000 metres along the north coast of Iwo Jima and it had suffered 4292 casualties; around a third were killed or mortally wounded and the rest were wounded or evacuated with combat fatigue. To compensate for the losses, General Rockey ordered Colonel Waller to release 10 per cent of the men from 13th Marine Artillery Regiment to reinforce the infantry regiments; they were at the limit of their endurance.

## 3rd Division's Advance to the East Coast (D+15 to D+19)

General Erskine's Marines were advancing across Nature's own hell east of Airfield 3, enduring the heat and stench caused by sulphur bubbling up through fissures and crevices in the rocky ground. Although tanks were ideal for suppressing the Japanese positions, there were only a few natural trails through the rocks and they were littered with mines and covered by anti-tank guns. The Marines pushed on alone while the engineers and bulldozers cleared routes forward.

2/21st Battalion advanced early on 6 March and reached the summit of Hill 357 during the afternoon, giving Major Percy's Marines a commanding view of the east coast. RCT 9 attacked an hour later but it could not clear Hill 362-A. 3/9th Battalion made a surprise attack on Hill 362-A the following morning and

*Tanks struggled to find suitable routes across the rough landscape but were always very welcome when they could find a way through. This squad are escorting a tank dozer as it carves a route to the front line. (NARA-127-GW-114025)*

advanced through a smoke screen for 30 minutes before a burst of machine-gun fire alerted every Japanese soldier in the area. As the sky began to lighten, Lieutenant Colonel Boehm noticed that his leading company had only reached Hill 331; Hill 362-A was another 250 metres to the southeast. He had been sent in the right direction but towards the wrong objective.

All Boehm could do was to organise a new attack, only this time the Japanese were waiting and his Marines came under fire from all sides. Although progress was slow and casualties were high, 3/9th Battalion captured Hill 362-C before nightfall. Lieutenant Colonel Boehm summed up the attack as follows:

> Most notable in the night attack was the fact that, although nearly all the basic dope was bad, the strategy proved very sound, since it turned out that the open ground taken under cover of darkness was the most heavily fortified of all terrain captured that day, and the enemy occupying this vital ground were taken completely by surprise (actually sleeping in their pillboxes and caves) … It should be kept in mind, however, that a stroke of luck went a long way toward making the attack a success.

RCT 9 renewed its attack at first light on 7 March but it had only advanced 200 metres when the Marines came under fire from all directions and became cut off. In 1st Battalion's sector, Second Lieutenant John H. Leims laid telephone lines across 400 metres of fire-swept ground before leading his men back to safety. He later returned twice in the dark to rescue wounded men. Leims was awarded the Medal of Honor. 2nd Battalion was also surrounded and although tanks managed to rescue Company E, Company F remained cut off until the following morning.

3rd Division spent 8 March clearing the east coast and while RCT 21 cleared the cliff tops, a destroyer fired directly into the ravines below. In RCT 9's sector Japanese soldiers were gathering to make a last stand east of Motoyama village, in an area known as Cushman's Pocket after 2/9th Battalion's commanding officer.

*These two Marines have just helped clear the pillbox in the background and they are waiting to move out towards their next objective. (NARA-127-GW-113803)*

Neither 3/21st not 2/9th Battalions could make any progress down the ravines on 9 March but patrols from both 1/21 and 3/9th Battalions reached the shoreline. 1/21st Battalion's patrol was the first to the beach and the intelligence officer sent a canteen filled with sea water to the corps commander with a note; 'For inspection, not consumption.' It was just what General Schmidt wanted to hear. Japanese resistance had been light but General Erskine still ordered his battalions to dig in along the cliffs for the night; the general advance to the eastern shoreline could wait until morning.

The following morning 1st Battalion reached the beach in RCT 21's sector, however, 3rd Battalion ran into difficulties when a disabled Sherman tank came to life. An enterprising Japanese soldier had climbed inside and worked out how to operate its turret and gun. After knocking out one tank he held up 3rd Battalion until a bazooka team crawled forward to silence him.

In RCT 9's sector, both 3rd and 1st Battalions advanced down the ravines and then linked up on the beach. Although General Erskine was able to report that 3rd Division's zone was free of organised resistance, it would take another six days to clear the remaining pockets of resistance along the cliffs. The delay was in part due to the large number of replacements that the division had absorbed. There was no time for small unit training and their inexperience led to many needless casualties.

## 4th Division Takes Minami and Higashi (D+15 to D+19)

General Cates' high hopes for a fresh attack on 6 March were quickly dashed as noted in the division's operations report: 'The results of fatigue and lack of experienced leaders is very evident in the manner in which the units fight.' RCT 23 hardly moved while RCT 24 had done little to increase its stranglehold on the Turkey Knob.

Cates changed his plans for 7 March; he would use a hammer and anvil strategy to crack the Meat Grinder while RCT 23 pushed for the coast. RCT 24 would hammer the Turkey Knob from northeast while the rest of RCT 25 hammered it from the southeast. 3/25th Marines formed the anvil west of the Amphitheatre, laying mines and erecting booby trapped barbed wire fences to stop the Japanese escaping. Machine guns and three 37mm guns armed with canister shells were dug in and camouflaged; mortars were also registered to hit the area in front of Captain Headley's Marines.

Disaster struck in front of Higashi when a rocket exploded in 2/23rd Marines' command post before dawn; Major Davison and his executive officer, operations officer, adjutant and communications chief were all casualties. Lieutenant Colonel Dillon took over but 2nd Battalion could only advance 150 metres. RCT 24 struggled to make progress towards Higashi. RCT 25 also failed to advance southeast of the Meat Grinder. By the end of the day it was clear to General Cates that both his flanks had to hammer harder if they were going to drive the Japanese onto his anvil.

*The Japanese feared the flamethrower and their snipers kept a lookout for the distinctive shape of the fuel pack and nozzle. (NARA-127-GW-111006)*

4th Division made a surprise pre-dawn attack on 8 March but the Marines only moved a short distance before the Japanese were alerted and a day of bitter fighting followed. Although Cates did not know it, Captain Inoue, the Iwo Naval Land Force Commander, was killed in the fighting around Higashi.

Since 1 March the division intelligence officer had warned that the risk of counterattacks would rise as the Japanese were pushed back to the coast: 'POW interrogation reveals general counterattacks are discouraged by Jap commanders as long as gun and mortar positions are intact. After permanent positions have been overrun by Blue troops, counterattacks are to be made at the discretion of unit commanders.' He was about to be proved right.

An unusual amount of mortar, rocket and artillery fire hit 4th Division's lines during the night of 8/9 March; it was being used to mask the sounds of 310th Independent Infantry Battalion's 1st Company creeping through RCT 23's lines. The troops were well equipped and while many carried demolition charges, some carried stretchers and planned to shout 'Corpsman' when they were spotted to fool the Marines. Shortly before midnight, shouts and screams signalled the alarm as 2/23rd Marines came under attack and Lieutenant Colonel Dillon's men were fighting for their lives.

The support ships lit the night sky with star shells while Company E fought to hold its position. A jeep with a trailer loaded with grenades and mortar shells saved the day when ammunition

*After the Japanese counterattack on the night of 8 March, RCT 23 moves out with fixed bayonets to check the area north of Higashi. (NARA-127-GW-142979)*

began to run out. Dillon's Marines survived the night and at sunrise the Japanese withdrew. Mopping up continued until noon and around 800 Japanese dead were counted in 4th Division's line, the majority around Company E; many more were later found in No Man's Land.

Japanese resistance reduced after the counterattack and 4th Division was about to take its revenge. While 2/23rd Marines could not advance far on the left flank, 3/24th Marines overcame the strongpoint covering Higashi village and advanced 300 metres towards Tachiiwa Point. The breakthrough released 1/24th and 1/25th Marines and they swung round to increase the stranglehold on the Turkey Knob.

10 March marked the last coordinated corps and divisional artillery barrage on Iwo Jima because Japanese-held areas had become too small to target with anything larger than mortars. On 4th Division's right flank, 2/23rd and 3/24th Marines advanced quickly past Higashi, leaving enemy strongpoints for infantry-engineer-tank teams to clear out with flamethrowers and demolitions. By mid afternoon, patrols were at the coast either side of Tachiiwa Point, having advanced over 1000 metres. Colonel Wensiger's objective had been taken earlier than expected and the rapid advance was attributed to the number of Japanese killed during the previous night's counterattack.

Meanwhile, RCT 25 continued to close in on the Turkey Knob and this time 3rd and 2nd Battalions made contact on the far side around noon and had secured the hilltop bunker by nightfall. 1st Battalion also destroyed the final pocket of resistance in the area. After two weeks of bitter fighting, General Cates was pleased to report that the Meat Grinder had finally been taken. Although organised resistance was over in 4th Division's sector, it would take another six days before the area was secure.

4th Division suffered 4075 casualties between 25 February and 10 March in the Meat Grinder: nearly 850 killed or mortally wounded and over 3000 wounded or evacuated with combat fatigue. It left battalions short of men and companies were

# CLEANING UP

Lieutenant Colonel Melvin L. Krulewitch gathered over 400 officers and men under his command and they set to work checking out the caves and bunkers behind 4th Division's front. It would take three days to mop up the rear areas and Krulewitch's temporary unit then disbanded, its work done.

frequently exchanged to support assaults. In RCT 24, 1st and 2nd Battalions had to disband one company each because they had fewer than 150 men. 4th Division was also getting close to breaking point.

With the end of organised Japanese resistance in sight, important command changes took place to accommodate the expansion of the airfield and base facilities on Iwo Jima. Brigadier General Ernest C. Moore of VII Fighter Command became the island's Air Commander on 6 March. He also assumed command of 15th Fighter Group with 47th Fighter Squadron's 28 P-51s (Mustangs) and 548th Night Fighter Squadron's 12 P-61s (Black Widows). Major General James E. Chaney assumed his dual role as Commanding General, Army Garrison Forces, and Island Commander, Iwo Jima, the following day, taking responsibility for three things. Firstly, he would oversee control of the airfields;

## Marine Casualties, 25 February–10 March

|  | Killed | Died of wounds | Missing | Wounded | Fatigue | Total |
|---|---|---|---|---|---|---|
| 5th Division | 830 | 263 | 5 | 2974 | 220 | 4292 |
| 3rd Division | 627 | 200 | 4 | 2241 | 491 | 3563 |
| 4th Division | 642 | 205 | 1 | 2836 | 301 | 4075 |

secondly, he would coordinate the island's air defences; thirdly, he would direct the development of Iwo Jima's base facilities.

There were also several changes off shore. When the island-based 15th Fighter Group took over combat air patrol duties on 8 March the carrier planes were stood down and USS *Enterprise*'s carrier fleet headed for Ulithi. On 9 March the *Eldorado* left for Guam with Admiral Turner and his staff on board, while General Smith's command post transferred to the *Auburn*. The Joint Expeditionary Force, Amphibious Support Force, Attack Force, Gunfire and Covering Force and Expeditionary Troops were reorganised as Task Group 51.21 under Admiral Hill, the Senior Officer Present Afloat.

# THE FINAL PHASE (D+20 TO D+35)

By 11 March the battle was entering its final stages and while 5th Division still had some ground to cover along the north coast, 3rd and 4th Divisions only had to clear a few final pockets of resistance. Even so there was still a lot of hard fighting ahead and the Marines could not count on artillery, air and naval support because the Japanese were in such small areas.

The heavy cruisers *Tuscaloosa* and *Salt Lake City* fired their final salvo on 12 March, although destroyers did continue to fire illumination shells until the 24th. The P-51 Mustangs of 15th Fighter Group flew their last combat support mission on 14 March while the Marine artillery ceased fire two days later. From then on the Marines would have to fight on with only their tanks and halftracks to help them.

Although 5th Division had secured the west side of Kitano's Gorge, it would take until 16 March before RCT 26 had secured the east side, including Hill 165 and Kitano Point, the northern point of the island. RCT 27 had cleared the cliffs with the help of 1/21st Marines by 15 March, securing everywhere but the gorge in 5th Division's area.

During 2/26th Marines' fight to reach the ravine, Private Franklin E. Sigler took command when his leader was hit and led his squad towards a Japanese position, annihilating the crew with grenades.

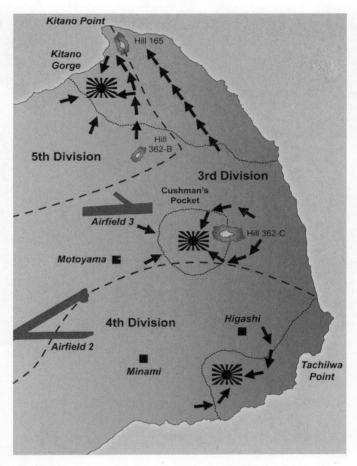

*Clearing the last pockets of resistance, D+20 to D+25 (11–16 March).*

When they came under fire from the caves above, Sigler climbed the rocks and engaged the Japanese, only to be severely wounded. He returned to his company and continued to direct machine-gun and rocket barrages on caves. Sigler even carried three wounded squad members to safety and had to be ordered to retire for medical treatment; he was awarded the Medal of Honor.

*RCT amassed a large armoury of captured weapons and equipment during the clearing of Cushman's Pocket. (NARA-127-GW-113119)*

As mentioned earlier, to the south 3rd Division had two pockets of resistance left to clear by 11 March, the cliff tops and 'Cushman's Pocket' southwest of Hill 362C, named after Lieutenant Colonel Robert E. Cushman, 2/9th Marines' commanding officer. Colonel Kenyon planned a pincer attack to stop the Japanese escaping from the pocket and while his 3rd Battalion formed the left hook, 1st Battalion made the right hook. Both advanced with the help of Sherman tanks and by mid afternoon Cushman's Pocket was surrounded.

At the same time 3/21st Marines attacked the southwest corner of the Pocket and it had an innovative weapon to help it. Several 7.2-inch rocket launchers designed for the M4A2 Sherman had been brought to Iwo Jima but the mechanics had discovered that they would not fit the new M4A3 tanks. Each launcher had 20

## THE NIGHT WATCH

Sometimes the Marine engineers and infantrymen worked all day long, destroying pillboxes and caves, with hardly a shot being fired. At night the Japanese crawled out of their caves and tunnels to throw grenades before disappearing back underground. Marine snipers kept a sharp look out for these night raiders, shooting many before they could cause any harm.

rocket tubes and they could fire 640 pounds of explosive to a range of 250 yards. The tank maintenance teams had mounted four on sleds. One launcher was dragged to the front by a tank and although it fired ten devastating salvos, 3/21st Marines could not advance through the maze of Japanese-held caves and spider traps.

RCT 9 continued the attack on Cushman's Pocket with 1st and 3d Battalions attacking the east side while 3/21st continued to act as the anvil on the opposite side. Engineers worked with an armoured bulldozer to clear a road through the maze of rocky outcrops for the tanks and flame tanks, so the Marines could guide them towards the Japanese hideouts. Cushman's Pocket was finally cleared on 14 March with the help of the last airstrikes of the campaign, ending organised resistance in 3rd Division's area. Now it could turn north to help 5th Division deal with the last Japanese-held area.

## RCT 21 Advances to Kitano Point (D+25)

On 16 March 3rd Division took over 5th Division's right flank and RCT 21 advanced northwest behind the final naval barrage fired against Iwo. While 1st Battalion moved quickly along the coast, 2nd Battalion had to clear out many caves and spider holes as it closed in on Kitano Point. Occasionally Japanese soldiers broke cover and made a Kamikaze run towards a tank or group of Marines armed

## NO TIME TO LEARN

By this stage of the battle, most of the Marine battalions had absorbed a large number of infantry replacements to replace casualties. While these men had been through training, they lacked combat experience and many were killed or injured before they could gain any. Unit efficiency suffered due to the high attrition rates. Casualties would have been much higher but for the help given by the flamethrower Shermans and the armoured bulldozers.

with demolition charges or grenades; most were shot down before they made contact. By early afternoon General Erskine was pleased to report that the north-east coast of Iwo Jima was clear.

## 4th Division's Clears Tachiiwa Point (D+20 to D+25)

By 11 March 4th Division faced its last pocket of Japanese resistance based in a maze of scrub-covered crevices and rocky outcrops to the south of Higashi village. Although RCT 23 was able to advance to the coast around Tachiiwa point and cover all beach areas, RCT 25 was unable to make any progress against the west side of the pocket. In the afternoon, a Japanese prisoner reported that he knew of 300 well armed troops in caves and tunnels and while they had plenty of ammunition and water, they had little food. He also told the interrogator that there was a Japanese general down there with them and it was assumed that he was Major General Senda, commanding 2nd Mixed Brigade.

Early the following morning a surrender appeal was broadcast to General Senda and the morning's attack was postponed while the prisoner led a Marine patrol towards the brigade commander's supposed hideout. After two hours of trying to start the amplifier's generator the patrol returned and RCT 25's attack went ahead.

*Marines try to coax a wounded Japanese soldier out of his dugout. More often than not they chose suicide over surrender. (NARA-127-GW-111384)*

2nd Battalion advanced slowly down the ravines toward the coast supported by tanks and flame tanks while the rest of the regiment gave supporting fire. The area was so small that artillery, airstrikes and naval support could not be used and the Marines had to clear position after position with flamethrowers, bazookas, rifles, grenades and demolitions. The engineers followed, clearing a road through the rocks so that the flame tanks could get closer to the action. Time after time the Marines tried to entice trapped soldiers to surrender only to be answered with sniper or machine-gun fire.

And so it continued for the next four days, advancing on average only five metres an hour, squeezing the Japanese pocket until the break came on the night of 15 March. A large group of Japanese troops attempted to infiltrate the Marine lines, hoping to cause as much damage as they could, but they were spotted and cut down before they could get far.

*All is not as it seems. The volcanic rock on Iwo Jima was soft enough to carve with a sharp knife and enterprising Japanese soldiers had sculptured this model of a tank to draw fire away from their bunker. (NARA-111-SC-208998)*

RCT 25 cleared the pocket the following morning and with the battle over, Colonel Lanigan's Marines were able to relax and reflect on what they had been through. During the final sweep of the pocket, Corpsman Francis J. Pierce was on a reconnaissance mission when he saw two stretcher bearer parties hit by machine-gun fire. He gave covering fire for those who could escape while administering aid to those wounded. After winning the fire fight, he carried the two wounded men to safety. Pierce was wounded while aiding an injured Marine the following day but again he continued to giving covering fire; he was awarded the Medal of Honor.

Further investigations revealed that the prisoner had been correct about General Senda; he had moved his brigade headquarters from the east of Hill 382 down to Higashi a few days earlier. However, the prisoner was incorrect about the number of Japanese in the area. 4th Division reckoned Senda had around 1500 army and navy troops under his command. Many of them were dead, scattered across the Iwo Jima's battered landscape, or buried in caves and tunnels. Many more were still in hiding, waiting for an opportune moment to strike; hardly any had been taken prisoner.

## To Kitano Point (D+20 to D+25)

On 11 and 12 March, 5th Marine Division advanced the final few yards up the ridge that had dominated its advance for the past few days. Once at the crest, they could go no further because they were faced with a steep-sided gorge and both sides had to be taken before it could be entered. General Rockey's intelligence officer estimated that around 1000 Japanese troops were hidden in the caves in front of them and 'there is no shortage of manpower, weapons, or ammunition in the area the Japanese have left to defend.' While RCT 28 held the west side of the ravine, RCT 27 mopped up resistance to the south of it using flame tanks, 'the one weapon that caused the Japanese to leave their caves and rock crevices and run.'

By 15 March two sides of the ravine were secure but General Rockey would have to wait for 3rd Division to clear the east side, for 5th Division was by now a shadow of the unit that had landed three weeks earlier. Battalions were only company strength while companies were platoon strength and few of the men who had stepped ashore on D-Day were still with their units. The replacements were not of the same quality as the veterans and many were killed or injured before they learned how to survive.

## NOT FORGOTTEN

Private George Phillips of 2/28th Marines was on night watch on 14 March when a hand grenade landed in the midst of his sleeping comrades. He shouted a warning and jumped on top of it; he was awarded the Medal of Honor for giving his life to save others.

## The Battle for Kitano Gorge (D+20 to D+35)

At 09:30 on 14 March the official flag raising ceremony took place at VAC Headquarters and as the new flag went up, the original flag which had flown over Suribachi since D-plus-4 was taken down. Shortly afterwards General Smith, the Commander of Expeditionary Troops, and his staff left Iwo Jima by air; they had commanded the largest Marine tactical force ever to engage an enemy. Two days later Iwo Jima was declared officially secure after 26 days of bitter fighting. On the same day Major General Senda, 2nd Mixed Brigade's commander, committed suicide.

By 16 March the only pocket of organised resistance was in Kitano Gorge, around 700 yards long and 300 yards wide, southwest of Kitano Point, where 500 Japanese soldiers were holding out under General Kuribayashi. While RCT 28 held the west side, RCT 26 had to take the east side and 1st Battalion had edged north to the coast, sealing off the ravine. The rest of RCT 26 cleared the area south of Kitano Point with the help of the final artillery preparation of the campaign.

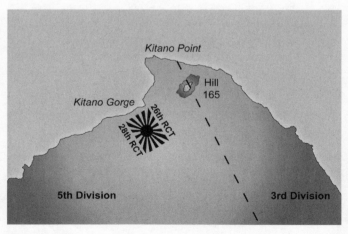

*General Kuribayashi's last stand in Kitano Gorge.*

For the next nine days RCT 26 edged its way round the rocky outcrops and down the narrow ravines while the Japanese fought back with rifles and machine guns. 5th Division's report describes the difficult descent into the ravine:

> In attacking these positions, no Japanese were to be seen, all being in caves or crevices in the rocks and so disposed as to give an all-around interlocking, ghost-like defense to each small compartment. Attacking troops were subjected to fire from flanks and rear more than from their front. It was always difficult and often impossible to locate exactly where defensive fires originated … When the position was overrun or threatened, the enemy retreated further into his caves where he usually was safe from gunfire, only to pop out again as soon as the occasion warranted unless the cave was immediately blown.

A huge igloo-shaped structure at the bottom of the ravine appeared to be the centre of resistance. Neither tank shells not demolition charges could penetrate the thick concrete. The Marines had to silence the surrounding positions while the engineers blasted a road down into the ravine so a bulldozer could get to the bunker. It then pushed earth and rocks against the structure's door, sealing the Japanese inside. Five explosives charges totalling 8500lbs were set and then detonated, blowing the bunker to pieces.

The loss of the bunker severely limited Japanese activity in the gorge and by evening of 24 March the pocket had been reduced to an area no more than 50 by 50 yards next to the sea. The following day RCT 28 took over the area and made the final attacks.

## The Final Days

During the final stages of the battle the Marines made many attempts to get the Japanese to give up, either individually or en masse. Almost all attempts failed; they preferred to fight to the

*Private First Class Glen Murphy is taking no chances with this bunker; he is firing a full clip of ammunition into this aperture before moving on. (NARA-127-GW-109920)*

death or commit suicide rather than surrender. Propaganda leaflets had been dropped from planes or stuffed into artillery shells and fired behind Japanese lines. Japanese-American language officers known as *Nisei* and POW volunteers had also used megaphones to shout instructions into bunkers and caves.

POWs reported that General Kuribayashi and his staff had moved to Colonel Ikeda's cave on 16 March. While General Erskine felt that neither General Kuribayashi nor Admiral Ichimaru could be induced to give up, it was worth trying to get a message to the Colonel. Two POWs equipped with a walkie-talkie were sent down into the gorge and after six hours they reported they had found Ikeda's cave. After giving him the message, they made their escape while the 3rd Division Language Section monitored their progress. It made no difference and some doubted they had met the Colonel.

On 17 March, Major Horie, commander of the Chichi Jima garrison, sent a message to Kuribayashi, confirming his promotion to full general; there was no reply. Four days later a single message reached Chichi Jima; 'We have not eaten nor drunk for five days. But our fighting spirit is still running high. We are going to fight bravely till the last.' There were another three days of silence and then one final message; 'All officers and men of Chichi Jima, goodbye.'

No one knows what happened to General Kuribayashi but it can be assumed that he either died in combat or committed suicide rather than be captured. A few believe that he led a breakout by 250 Japanese, many of them officers and senior non-commissioned officers, early on 26 March. They infiltrated 5th Division's lines before dawn and attacked the bivouacs near the western beaches.

First Lieutenant Harry L. Martin of the 5th Pioneer Battalion organised a firing line with the Marines nearest his foxhole and stopped the Japanese in their tracks. On hearing that several men were trapped and in danger, he worked his way forward and although badly wounded he found them and directed them to safety. When a group of Japanese showered his men with grenades, Martin killed them all with only a pistol. Rather than wait for another attack he led his own, dispersing the Japanese. Martin was mortally wounded stopping the Japanese attack and was posthumously awarded the Medal of Honor.

5th Pioneer Battalion eventually stopped the Japanese infiltrating farther but it took the men of VII Fighter Command three hours to wipe them all out; Kuribayashi was not identified. None of the group was taken alive and the number of prisoners taken by V Amphibious Corps still only stood at 216.

The US casualties during the final phase were 3885, the majority suffered in Kitano Gorge.

| | Killed in action | Died of wounds | Wounded | Missing | Total |
|---|---|---|---|---|---|
| 3rd Division | 147 | 60 | 505 | 53 | 765 |
| 4th Division | 139 | 87 | 442 | 52 | 720 |
| 5th Division | 467 | 168 | 1640 | 122 | 2400 |

# THE LEGACY

## Leaving Iwo Jima Behind

4th Division started to leave the island as early as 14 March and sailed for Maui. Five days later the last of General Erskine's Marines stepped off Iwo Jima's beaches. 5th Division and corps troops started loading out on 18 March and headed for Hawaii, an operation that lasted ten days. It left 3rd Marine Division (less 3rd Marines) behind to take over patrol and defence responsibilities until 147th Infantry arrived from New Caledonia on 20 March. Between them they carried out day patrols and set night ambushes of various sizes to protect installations against prowling Japanese.

The completion of the Iwo Jima operation was formally announced at 08:00 on 26 March and Commander Forward Area, Central Pacific, assumed responsibility for the defence and development of the island. Major General James E. Chaney also took over operational control of all units stationed on the island while Brigadier General Ernest Moore assumed the designation of Air Defense Commander. While General Schmidt left Iwo Jima by air, his headquarters embarked on USS *President Monroe*.

3rd Division began loading on 27 March and assumed full responsibility for ground defence on 4 April. Although the last Marine unit left Iwo Jima on 12 April, the fighting was not over;

hundreds of Japanese were still hiding in caves and tunnels across the island. Many would commit suicide or die from their untreated wounds but others waited for their moment to strike at the Americans. In April and May the 147th Infantry captured 867 prisoners and killed around 1600 in skirmishes across the island.

## The Cost

The Battle of Iwo Jima cost over 26,000 American casualties, including 6800 dead, and it was the only US Marine battle where the American casualties exceeded those of the Japanese. However, of the 22,000 Japanese soldiers on the island it was believed that over 21,000 died from fighting or ritual suicide so the number of deaths tripled the American fatalities. It was believed that only about 300 Japanese were left alive in the caves and tunnels and they stayed there due to the combination of their *Bushido* code of honour and effective anti-American propaganda. They would only emerge at night to look for provisions and when they were captured or surrendered they were surprised to be treated well. Two men lasted six years underground (some sources say four years). In the end nearly 3000 were rounded up. Only two Marines were captured during the battle and neither survived captivity.

## The Battle for Okinawa

General Simon Buckner's Tenth US Army had been training for the invasion of the Ryukyu Islands for some time but preparations intensified as soon as Iwo Jima was captured. Okinawa was just south of the Japanese mainland and it had been chosen as the staging area for an invasion. Since the summer of 1944 Japanese troops had been pouring onto the island to build fortifications and by March 1945 they were ready for the imminent amphibious attack. As 77th Division cleared the outlying islands in preparation for the main assault, there was no doubt about it; Operation *Iceberg* was going to be a costly campaign.

*Tenth Army's landings on Okinawa required a massive flotilla. While landing craft and amphibious vehicles ferried troops and supplies from the landing ships to the beach, destroyers kept a watchful eye for Japanese planes.*

On 1 April, Task Force 56, a fleet of ten battleships, nine cruisers, 23 destroyers and over 100 rocket gunboats opened fire at the start of L-Day, in what was the heaviest concentration of naval gunfire ever used during an amphibious invasion. As shells hit the shoreline, hundreds of landing craft and amphibious vehicles carried two Army divisions and two Marine divisions towards Hagushi beaches on the west side of the island while simulated amphibious landings off the southeast coast kept General Ushijima guessing. His decision to defend the interior of the island meant that Tenth US Army was able to put over 60,000 men ashore by nightfall for a handful of casualties; it was the calm before the storm.

7th Division and 1st Marine Division advanced quickly across the island, cutting Ushijima's forces in two. The majority of his troops were holding the Shuri Line to the south and General Simon Buckner ordered 6th Marine Division to drive north up the Ishikawa Isthmus while the rest of Tenth Army deployed. It found the main Japanese concentration in wooded ravines on the Motobu Peninsula and it took over two weeks to clear the area.

While Tenth US Army advanced across Okinawa the Japanese Navy Air Service struck back, making kamikaze and conventional air attacks against Task Force 51's warships and landing craft. A final attempt to engage the US Navy on 6 April ended in disaster when an American submarine spotted the super battleship *Yamato* leaving Kyushu; aircraft from Task Force 58's carriers intercepted it and sank the pride of the Japanese Navy.

Meanwhile, XXIV Corps attacked the ridges and hills covering the Outer Shuri Line on 5 April and while 96th Division fought for Cactus Ridge, 7th Division captured the Pinnacle. The advance stalled on Kakazu Ridge, in front of the Main Shuri Line but Buckner's men kept pushing forward in a bloody battle of endurance.

After clearing Motobu Peninsula, 77th Division landed on the island of Ie Shima off the northwest coast of Okinawa on 16 April and cleared it after a week of heavy fighting. It allowed US engineers to build a runway on the tiny island, turning it into a base for air attacks against Okinawa.

On the mainland, XXIV Corps was still struggling to make progress and the addition of an extra division to the American line was making little difference. A renewed attack against Kakazu Ridge on 19 April failed and the GIs and Marines had to rely on explosives and flamethrowers to burn or blast their way across Skyline Ridge and Tombstone Ridge. General Buckner referred to these new tactics as the 'blowtorch and corkscrew' method.

One by one the hills and ridges of the Outer Shuri Line were cleared. By the end of April, XXIV Corps had reorganised just in time to meet General Ushijima's counterattack on 4 May. As 32nd Army's infantry, tanks and artillery fought to regain the Outer Shuri Line, kamikaze aircraft and boats sank seventeen American ships. Japanese casualties were enormous and 7th Division struck back, clearing Maeda Escarpment on 7 May.

The attack against the Inner Shuri Line began on 11 May and while the first breakthrough came two days later, heavy rains

*The Japanese Air Force struck back at the fleet anchored off Okinawa on 6 April. The sky is dotted with anti-aircraft fire as a pilot aims his burning plane towards an aircraft carrier.*

prevented XXIV Corps from moving forward. The delay allowed the Japanese troops to withdraw from the ruins of Shuri and Naha to the Yaeju-Dake Escarpment at the south end of the island.

While XXIV Corps pushed forward, 6th Marine Division landed on the Oroku Peninsula, bypassing the main Japanese line. Ushijima refused to surrender and committed suicide on 22 June (General Buckner had been killed in action). Hundreds of Japanese soldiers followed their leader's example rather than surrender and as XXIV Corps cleared out the last pockets of resistance, the bloodiest campaign in the Pacific finally came to an end on 2 July 1945. While Tenth Army had suffered 62,000 casualties (12,000 of them killed or missing), 95,000 Japanese troops on Okinawa died defending the island; only 7400 were captured. Civilian casualties have been estimated at anywhere between 50,000 and 150,000.

## The Atomic Bomb

The Philippine and Okinawa campaigns ended at the beginning of July but thousands of Japanese soldiers were still holding out in the mountains and jungles. After the horrendous losses on Okinawa, the prospect of attacking mainland Japan was terrible and as the Soviet Army planned to intervene in the war against Japan, the United States' new President, Harry S Truman, wanted a speedy conclusion to the war in the Pacific.

The US Navy proposed to force a Japanese surrender through a total naval blockade and air raids, and Japan's inland and coastal waterways were mined by air under Operation *Starvation*. Strategic bombing also increased under the command of General Curtis LeMay and around half of the built-up areas of 64 cities were destroyed by fire bombing, drastically reducing Japanese industrial production. It is estimated that 100,000 people were killed in air raids over Tokyo on 9 and 10 March alone.

One possible solution was provided on 16 July. For some time the Allies had been striving to harness nuclear energy and the successful testing of an atomic weapon at Alamogordo, New Mexico, gave the American President the answer, albeit a terrifying one. The Potsdam Declaration of 26 July, calling for Japan's immediate and unconditional surrender, was made with the knowledge that atomic weapons could be unleashed. The Japanese High Command refused, setting the scene for the dawning of a new age of warfare, the nuclear age.

Whether the decision to carry out the atomic bombings was the right one has long been debated. While some experts believed the bombing raids and naval blockade had undermined Japan's ability to wage war, others argued that the use of the atomic bomb cancelled the need for what would have been a very costly invasion, both in military and civilian casualties.

On the morning of 6 August *Enola Gay*, a B-29 Superfortress piloted by Colonel Paul Tibbets, flew over the port of Hiroshima

*Thousands of men, women and children died in an instant when the atomic bomb exploded over Hiroshima; thousands more would die over the years that followed.*

at the southern end of the Japanese mainland. It dropped a single bomb codenamed 'Little Boy' and as Tibbets turned his plane for home, the bomb exploded at 2000 feet. 'A bright light filled the plane, we turned back to look at Hiroshima. The city was hidden by that awful cloud … boiling up, mushrooming.'

The explosion burnt everything in its path while strong winds demolished virtually everything within a three-kilometre radius. Thousands were killed or seriously injured but worse was to come; radiation sickness affected many of the survivors and estimates put the death toll over the first twelve months at more than 140,000.

Three days later a second atomic bomb, codenamed 'Fat Man', was dropped on the nearby city of Nagasaki with the same devastating effects. One the same day, the one-million strong Soviet Army invaded Manchuria as agreed with President Roosevelt back in March.

While the Japanese Supreme War Council considered the Allies' demands to surrender, some commanders were determined to die defending their homeland. On 10 August the Japanese Cabinet accepted the Potsdam terms and five days later Emperor Hirohito broadcast to the nation and to the world that his people would to 'bear the unbearable'; Imperial Japan would surrender. 15 August would become known as 'V-J Day' (Victory in Japan) in English-speaking nations.

Allied warships sailed into Tokyo harbour on 28 August and on the morning of 2 September General Douglas MacArthur met the Japanese envoys on the deck of the USS *Missouri*; at four minutes past nine o'clock the war in the Pacific came to an end. MacArthur announced the news to the world: 'Today the guns are silent. A great tragedy has ended. A great victory has been won.'

# ORDERS OF BATTLE

## US Marines

### Expeditionary Troops (TF 56)

Lieutenant General Holland M. Smith

### V Amphibious Corps (VACLF)

Major General Harry Schmidt

### 3rd Marine Division (Major General Graves B. Erskine)

3rd Marines: 1st/2nd/3rd Battalions (Colonel James A. Stuart)
9th Marines: 1st/2nd/3rd Battalions (Colonel Howard N. Kenyon)
21st Marines: 1st/2nd/3rd Battalions (Colonel Hartnoll J. Withers)
12th Marines (artillery): 1st/2nd/3rd/4th Battalions (Lieutenant
Colonel Raymond F. Crist Jr)

Combat Support Units
3rd Tank Battalion
3rd Engineer Battalion
3rd Pioneer Battalion

Support Units
Service Troops, 3rd Service Battalion
3rd Motor Transport Battalion
3rd Medical Battalion

## 4th Marine Division (Major General Clifton B. Cates)

23rd Marines: 1st/2nd/3rd Battalions (Colonel Walter W. Wensinger)
24th Marines: 1st/2nd/3rd Battalions (Colonel Walter I. Jordan)
25th Marines: 1st/2nd/3rd Battalions (Colonel John R. Lanigan)
14th Marines (artillery): 1st/2nd/3rd/4th Battalions (Colonel Louis G. De Haven)

Combat Support Units
4th Tank Battalion
4th Engineer Battalion
4th Pioneer Battalion
5th and 10th Amphibian Tractor Battalions

Support Units
Service Troops, 4th Service Battalion
4th Motor Transport Battalion
4th Medical Battalion

## 5th Marine Division (Major General Keller E. Rockey)

26th Marines: 1st/2nd/3rd Battalions (Colonel Chester B. Graham)
27th Marines: 1st/2nd/3rd Battalions (Colonel Thomas A. Wornham)
28th Marines: 1st/2nd/3rd Battalions (Colonel Harry B. Liversedge)
13th Marines (artillery): 1st/2nd/3rd/4th Battalions (Colonel Louis G. De Haven)

Combat Support Units
5th Tank Battalion
5th Engineer Battalion
5th Pioneer Battalion
3rd and 11th Amphibian Tractor Battalions

Support Units
Service Troops, 5th Service Battalion
5th Motor Transport Battalion
5th Medical Battalion

## V Amphibious Corps (and major attached units)

Corps Troops, HQ and Service Battalion

Artillery and Anti-aircraft
1st Provisional Field Artillery Group
   2nd and 4th 155mm Howitzer Battalions
1338th Anti-Aircraft Group
   506th Anti-Aircraft Gun and 483rd AAAW Battalions

Logistics
Provisional LVT Group
8th Field Depot

Communications
Landing Force Air Support Control Unit
Signal Battalion, Provisional Signal Group

Medical
V Corps Medical Battalion
Corps Evacuation Hospital Number 1
38th Field Hospital, Reinforced (USA)

*Marines Memorial, Arlington Cemetery, recreating the celebrated photograph by Joe Rosenthal of the flag raising on Mount Suribachi.*

Engineers
2nd Separate Engineer Battalion
23rd, 31st, 62nd, 133rd Naval Construction Battalions
2nd Armored Amphibian Battalion

# Japanese Army

## 109th Division (General Tadamichi Kuribayashi)

2nd Mixed Brigade (Major General Sadasue Senda)
309th Battalion (Captain Awatsu)
310th Battalion (Major Iwatani)
311th Battalion (Major Tatsumi)
312th Battalion (Captain Osada)
314th Battalion (Captain Hakuda)
Engineer Battalion and Field Hospital

145th Infantry Regiment (Colonel Masuo Ikeda)
1st Battalion (Major Hara)
2nd Battalion (Major Yasutake)
3rd Battalion (Major Anso)
Engineer Company and Field Hospital

3rd Battalion, 17th Mixed Infantry Regiment (Major Tamachi Fujiwara)

Brigade Artillery Group (Colonel Kaido)
2nd Mixed Brigade's Artillery battalion
145th Infantry's artillery battalion
1st and 2nd Medium Mortar Battalions
20th Independent Artillery Mortar Battalion
8th, 9th, 10th, 11th and 12th Independent Anti-Tank Battalions
20th, 21st, 43rd and 44th Machine Cannon Units

Remnants of the 26th Tank Regiment (Lieutenant Colonel Nishi)
1st and 2nd Independent Machine-Gun Battalions
Three Army Rocket Units

## Naval Forces on Iwo Jima (Rear Admiral Ichimaru)

27th Air Flotilla and 2d Air Attack Force (Rear Admiral Ichimaru)
Iwo Jima Naval Guard Force (Captain Inoue)
125th, 132nd, 141st and 149th Naval Guard Force Anti-aircraft
Batteries
Naval Guard Force Coast Defense Batteries
Southern Air Group Naval Guard Force troops (Captain Inoue)
204th Naval Construction Battalion

# FURTHER READING

Batley, Lieutenant Colonel Whitman S., *Iwo Jima: Amphibious Epic* (USMC, Historical Section, Division of Public Information, Headquarters, US Marine Corps, 1954)

Bradley, James and Ron Powers, *Flags of Our Fathers* (Bantam, 2006)

Garand, George W. and Truman R. Strobridge, *History of US Marine Corps Operations in World War II, Vol IV: Western Pacific Operations, Part VI: Iwo Jima* (Historical Division Headquarters, US Marine Corps, 1971)

Hammel, Eric, *Iwo Jima: Portrait of a Battle: United States Marines at War in the Pacific* (Zenith Press, 2006)

Haynes, Major General Fred and James A. Warren, *The Lions of Iwo Jima* (Holt Paperbacks, 2009)

Kakehashi, Kumiko, *So Sad to Fall in Battle: An Account of War Based on General Tadamichi Kuribayashi's Letters from Iwo Jima* (Presidio Press, 2007)

Newcomb, Richard F. and Harry Schmidt, *Iwo Jima* (Holt Paperbacks, 2002)

Smith, Larry, *Iwo Jima: World War II Veterans Remember the Greatest Battle of the Pacific* (Norton & Company, 2008)

Wheller, Richard and Richard Wheeler, *Iwo* (US Naval Institute Press, 1994)

## Websites

http://www.defense.gov/home/features/iwo_jima/index.html
http://www.ibiblio.org/hyperwar/PTO/Iwo/index.html
http://www.marines.mil/news/publications/
Pageswesternpacificoperationshistoryofusmarinecorpsoperations
inworldwariipt4.aspx
http://www.iwojima.com/

## Films and Documentaries

*Glamour Gal* (1945); a film about Marine artillery.

*To the Shores of Iwo Jima* (1945); a documentary produced by the United States Navy, Marine Corps and Coast Guard.

*Sands of Iwo Jima* (1949); a film starring John Wayne.

*The Outsider* (1961); Tony Curtis stars as Ira Hayes, one of the flag raisers.

*The World at War* (1973); episode 23 of the BBC documentary covers the Iwo Jima campaign.

*Flags of Our Fathers* (2006); a film directed by Clint Eastwood giving the American perspective, based on James Bradley's and Ron Powers' book of the same name.

*Letters from Iwo Jima* (2006); originally titled *Red Sun, Black Sand*, this film gives the Japanese perspective.

*The Pacific* (2010); part 8 of the HBO mini-series produced by Tom Hanks and Steven Spielberg includes a piece on Iwo Jima.

# INDEX

# Index

# Index